Harald Geißler

AI-Coaching

How to leverage AI in coaching and for coaching purposes

Springer

Harald Geißler
Hamburg, Deutschland

ISBN 978-3-658-49177-2 ISBN 978-3-658-49178-9 (eBook)
https://doi.org/10.1007/978-3-658-49178-9

This book is a translation of the original German edition "KI-Coaching" by Harald Geißler, published by Springer Fachmedien Wiesbaden GmbH in 2025. The translation was done with the help of an artificial intelligence machine translation tool. A subsequent human revision was done primarily in terms of content, so that the book will read stylistically differently from a conventional translation. Springer Nature works continuously to further the development of tools for the production of books and on the related technologies to support the authors.

This Springer imprint is published by the registered company Springer Fachmedien Wiesbaden GmbH, part of Springer Nature.
The registered company address is: Abraham-Lincoln-Str. 46, 65189 Wiesbaden, Germany
When you dispose of this product, please recycle the paper.

AI-Coaching

for Ursula
with many thanks for the extensive support
and the many good conversations

Contents

Introduction and Overview

Contents

H. Geissler, *AI-Coaching*,
https://doi.org/10.1007/978-3-658-49178-9_1

The present study addresses the question of how artificial intelligence (AI) information technology can be meaningfully used in and for coaching. The term "meaningfully" is intended in two ways: first, that the goals of the coachees are effectively achieved, and second, that it is examined to what extent and in what respect these goals are meaningful.

By contrast, the following will not address how AI can be used for the marketing and administration of coaching, such as for scheduling and invoicing, as well as for feedback management and coach-coachee matching, i.e., the task of assigning suitable coaches from a coach pool to coachees.

The formulation that the focus is on the use of AI in and for coaching suggests that there are two fundamental ways of using it: first, to use AI *within* coaching processes, i.e., to *integrate* AI into coaching processes, and second, to use AI as a *substitute for human coaches.*

The first of these two possibilities will hereafter be referred to as *triadic AI coaching,* because three parties are involved: coach, coachee, and AI, in such a way that coach and coachee integrate the AI into their interpersonal dialogue.

If, on the other hand, the coach is replaced by AI, we refer to this as *dyadic AI coaching.*

These two fundamental usage options can also be combined, for example, when coachees prepare coaching sessions with the help of dyadic AI coaching and then discuss the corresponding experiences and insights with their coaches, without the AI being used directly in these coaching sessions. This usage format can be described as *semi-triadic AI coaching.*

A review of the current literature reflecting on the possible uses of AI for and in coaching reveals that the technical systems or machines used are referred to in various ways, such as

- AI systems (Edenhausen 2024),
- chatbots (Clutterbuck 2022; Gengler et al. 2024; Stenzel 2024),
- AI assistants (Clutterbuck 2022, p. 372),
- high-end assistance chatbots (Stenzel 2024),
- AI coachbots (Passmore et al. 2024),
- AI coaching chatbots (Terblanche 2020; Terblanche et al. 2022a, b; Terblanche and Kidd 2022; Terblanche et al. 2024; Terblanche 2024a, b)
- AI coaches (ibid.),
- coaching chatbots (Rutschmann 2024a),
- AI coaching companions (Rutschmann 2024b),
- AI coaching systems (DiGirolamo 2024),
- Business Buddys AI (▶ https://www.business-buddy.ai/).

With regard to the technical systems to which these terms refer, two groups can be distinguished:

- *non-coaching-specific chatbots,* e.g., ChatGPT, Perplexity, Claude, etc., i.e., all-purpose AI systems developed for a relatively wide variety of different use cases and, on this basis, can also be used for and in coaching,
- and *coaching-specific AI agents,* such as Vici, Alpina, Business Buddy.AI, Rocky.AI, etc., i.e., AI systems developed specifically for coaching.

The following will show how the technical capabilities of coaching-specific AI agents and non-coaching-specific chatbots can be used for and in coaching, and what implications this has for the fundamental understanding and conceptual development of coaching. But first, let us take a brief look at the societal context of this development and its possibilities.

1.1 Artificial Intelligence – the Great Challenge of Our Society

Artificial intelligence is a subfield of information technology, that is, technology capable of receiving structured (textual, visual, and acoustic) *data* and systematically connecting them into *information* using stochastic, i.e., probability theory-based, *algorithms.* On this basis, statements can be generated that give their users, such as coachees and coaches, the impression of *insights* or *decisions* that are the result of conscious or cognitive processes. In reality, however, these are *statements without any consciousness*. For they are solely the product of the chosen algorithms and the training program that the AI underwent during its development phase using extensive datasets.

Against this background, the question arises as to whether AI is still a *tool* or already an *actor.* That is: What must we do or consider to ensure that AI remains a tool in the hands of humans, such as coachees and coaches—and how can we use it meaningfully? And what must we do or refrain from doing to prevent AI from becoming an *actor* that seduces us or dictates which goals and values we should pursue?

This is precisely the problem that Harari (2024, p. 11) has in mind when he draws a parallel between artificial intelligence and the *Sorcerer's Apprentice,* as described by Goethe in the poem of the same name, to warn against the danger of ever engaging with forces that, on the one hand, have fascinating capabilities, but on the other hand, carry the risk that one may not be able to control them sufficiently.

This problem characterizes the recent development of AI, which in recent years has been advancing at an exorbitant pace, increasingly permeating and shaping the most diverse areas of public life, business, culture, politics, leisure, and last but not least, coaching practice.

This dynamic is driven on the one hand by *euphoria* and *optimism.* An example of this is Rebecca Rutschmann, who, together with Anke Paulick, built one of the first AI coaching agents and, in a LinkedIn post titled "The Rise of Better Humans Through AI: A Personal Thinking Journey into Language and Understanding" (Rutschmann 2024a), states the following:

> » "Looking ahead, we must decide how to integrate AI into our lives responsibly and thoughtfully. Will AI help us become better human beings? The answer lies in how we choose to engage with this technology. By fostering a collaborative relationship with AI, we can harness its potential to enhance our understanding of the world and ourselves.

> In this ever-evolving landscape, the fusion of human creativity and AI innovation invites us to redefine what it means to be human. It challenges us to explore new dimensions of empathy, connection, and self-awareness. As we navigate this journey, let us use AI not only as a tool but as a catalyst for personal and collective growth.
> Ultimately, the future of AI and humanity is intertwined. Our approach to this relationship will shape the trajectory of both.“

While this statement is dominated by euphoric elements, others emphasize the dangers to which we may be exposing ourselves too naively (Lenz 2023; Zweig 2023). A prominent example is a BBC interview in which the world-renowned physicist Stephen Hawking expressed his concerns and fears as follows in 2014:

> “The development of full artificial intelligence could mean the end of the human race.”
> The context of this statement was a discussion about the potential advancement of speech technology, which Hawking himself used for communication. He argued that even simple forms of AI had already proven to be powerful, but the development of systems that could rival or surpass human intelligence could have catastrophic consequences for humanity.
> Hawking further explained: “It would take off on its own and redesign itself at an ever-increasing rate. Humans, who are limited by slow biological evolution, couldn't compete and would be superseded.”
> Hawking largely maintained these views on AI in the following years. Even in his last book, “Brief Answers to the Big Questions,” published after his death in 2018, he once again warned of the potential dangers of advanced artificial intelligence.
> (Source: Perplexity, accessed on 28.08.2024)

However, it is not only concerns and fears that preoccupy Hawking. He also sees great opportunities in AI. In particular, he envisions the potential for AI to “reverse damage to the natural world” and “eradicate poverty and disease.”

In his view, however, this requires that the risks be minimized through the following:

Technical measures

- Use of fairness algorithms and high-quality datasets to reduce bias
- Implementation of security measures such as sandboxing, firewalls, antivirus programs, and encryption
- Development of systems for anomaly detection and identity verification

Organizational measures

- Training AI developers and users on risks and ethical considerations
- Introduction of an effective AI risk management framework to identify, assess, and minimize risks
- Continuous monitoring and control of AI systems even after implementation

Regulatory approaches

- Development of regulations and guidelines for handling AI systems

- Promotion of research projects to identify and prevent AI misuse
- Convening interdisciplinary expert panels to assess AI developments in sensitive areas

Transparency and control
- Increasing the transparency of AI systems regarding data used, algorithms, and results
- Implementation of external audits by independent third parties
- Examination of commercial AI systems for potential misuse

Ethical considerations
- Integration of ethical principles such as fairness, privacy, and accountability into AI development
- Promotion of trust-building measures and public awareness

By combining these measures, a balanced approach can be created that both fosters the innovative potential of AI and effectively minimizes the associated risks.

(Source: Perplexity, accessed on 28.08.2024)

In order to concretely assess the dangers, opportunities, and risk mitigation measures mentioned by Hawking—and many others—it is necessary to clarify for what *purpose* the AI is being used. This is because it makes a significant difference,
- whether the AI is used by individuals, groups, and organizations for criminal purposes
- or for combating crime,
- whether the AI is used by those in power and political systems to stabilize their rule and propagate certain ideologies
- or for democratizing society and improving the common good, e.g., by reducing social tensions,
- and whether the AI—on the basis of the existing legal framework and voluntary self-regulation—is used for profit optimization
- or for addressing questions of meaning and ethical challenges.

These various purposes of use are reflected in different *fields of application.* For example, it makes a difference whether AI is used in the military, in politics, in business or culture, in non-profit organizations, in public administration, in associations and clubs, or in private life.

With regard to these different fields of application, the question also arises as to whether *coaching* does not, or could not, play a central key role here. After all, coachees also come from these various fields of practice, and the responsibility of coaching must therefore be to positively influence these fields of practice through the coachees.

These considerations ultimately challenge us to reflect on our *conception of humanity* (Geißler 2000, p. 161 ff.; Prange 1978) and to develop answers to the following questions:

Questions for us and our conception of humanity

What can AI do that humans cannot, or cannot do as well? And what can humans do that AI currently and in the future cannot do, because there are certain boundaries that AI fundamentally cannot cross?

In other words: What are the similarities and differences between human intelligence and artificial intelligence—and is it even justified to refer to so-called artificial intelligence as intelligence?

And:

To what extent can and must we take responsibility for the development and use of AI? How great are the risks, and what are the reasons for the risks that this may not succeed and that we increasingly become the addressees and victims of AI, which takes over leadership everywhere and increasingly determines our lives?

And what can we do concretely in the various fields of practice to take and assume responsibility for leadership in the development and use of AI?

1.2 Artificial Intelligence and Coaching: How do they fit Together?

1.2.1 First Overview

These questions challenge the theory and practice of *coaching* (Bachkirova and Kemp 2024; Norton et al. 2024) and have led to different positions and usage strategies. Looking at the entirety of current coaching theory and practice, a general picture emerges (see Fig. 1.1) that is currently characterized by two main aspects, namely

- first, that artificial intelligence is used in and for coaching both in the form of non-coaching-specific *chatbots,* such as ChatGPT, and in the form of coaching-specific *AI agents*,
- and second, that for these two options, a *dyadic use* is possible, characterized by coaches being replaced by coaching bots or AI agents, and a *triadic use,* in which coach and coachee deliberately integrate AI into the coaching process.

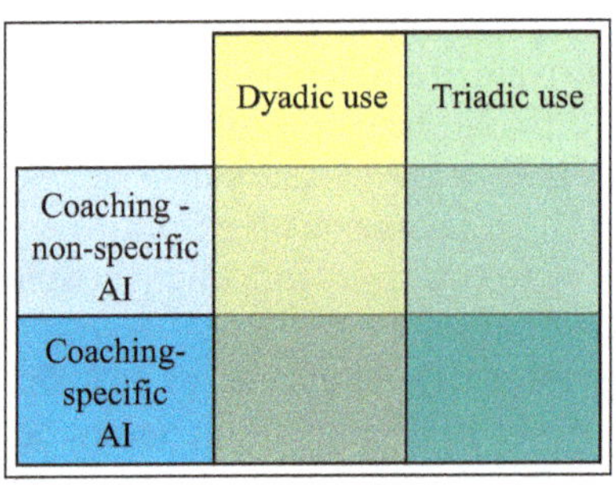

Fig. 1.1 The four possible uses of Artificial Intelligence in and for coaching

Based on this, if we ask how actively the various actors in coaching practice, academia, and coach education and training are currently using these four possibilities of Artificial Intelligence and driving the development of AI coaching both practically and conceptually, it becomes apparent that

- both coaches and coaching researchers, as well as those involved in coach education, training, and supervision, are currently engaging very little in the development of AI coaching and instead are limiting themselves to observing developments from a safe distance and with considerable skepticism (Diller et al. 2024).
- In comparison, (potential) coachees—i.e., people who have a problem that could be solved with coaching—are much more open to using Artificial Intelligence. With regard to them, it appears
  - that they are making extensive use of non-coaching-specific chatbots, such as ChatGPT, as a substitute for a coach
  - and are thus giving relatively strong impetus to the development of AI coaching.

Looking in detail at the development of coaching AI agents, the following can be observed with Rebecca Rutschmann (2024c):

- The early days of AI coaching companions can be seen as the convergence of two major forces: organizational demand for scalable, cost-effective coaching, and rapid advances in artificial intelligence. Early innovators such as **PocketConfidant, Rocky.ai, Evoach,** and **CoachVici** paved the way for AI chatbots designed to assist individuals in personal and professional growth.
- **PocketConfidant** founded by Olivier Malafronte pioneered AI Coaching from 2016 to 2023. The goal was to develop human capabilities in complex situations, avoid bias, and favor intelligence. They worked on fully automated natural language processing (NLP) techniques to play a meaningful role in transforming the coaching landscape.
- **CoachM** is a true digital coach for Lentity-value by Emma Weber created in 2017, increasing the impact of Learning Applications.
- **Rocky AI Coaching & Personal Development Platform,** founded early 2019 by Harry Novic, offered a Growth Mindset AI Coach also back in the days based on NLP (natural language processiong) techniques, which is now enhanced by generative AI. Now they offer both an AI Coach that offers personalized, daily coaching interactions to help users meet their goals, engage in daily reflection, and supports the development of soft skills and a white-label solution, allowing businesses to create branded coaching apps.
- **evoach,** founded mid 2019 by Rebecca Rutschmann and Anke Paulick, MBA, PCC (ICF), innovated by blending AI with decision-tree (scripted) approaches, including gamification focusing on personal development within organizations first. From 2021 to early 2022 they repivoted to offer a platform

for coaches to build their own coaching companions via a no-code builder. From 2022 fully integrating generative AI into their hybrid approach with the launch of their AI Coach Alpina in early March 2023, also used for different research papers.

- **CoachVici** or now AiCOACH Sp. z o.o., also founded in 2019 by Prof. Nicky Terblanche (PhD), used proven coaching and goal attainment theories to created first an only scripted chatbot, mainly for Nicky's research at first. Now Vici also incorporates generative AI models but is taking an organizational approach bridging the gaps between human-to-human coaching sessions by providing users with seamless, ongoing, and measurably effective goal-setting check-ins through the intuitive user interface.
- With **bestselfy,** Hilary Klassen and Moritz Krog started offering an AI-powered pocket coach that develops employees' soft-skills for higher individual and team performance in 2019. Now they are providing a complete Coaching toolbox and offering LeadershipLabs.
- These early AI Coaching providers set the stage for further advancements until 2020 by proving that AI could be used not just for transactional tasks (like scheduling and matchmaking) but also for reflective and growth-oriented conversations.

Finally, looking at the current coaching discourse, for example at the congress held in Zurich in September 2024, some turbulence is also apparent. While Nicky Terblanche emphasized the "democratization" of coaching made possible by replacing relatively expensive human coaches with extremely low-cost AI agents (Terblanche 2020; Terblanche et al.,2022a, b; Terblanche and Kidd 2022; Terblanche et al. 2024; Terblanche 2024a, b), Tatiana Bachkirova countered that human coaches can never be replaced by Artificial Intelligence. In her view, the communication skills of the AI agents used by Terblanche and others are at the level of *parrots who do not know what they are saying, because what they say has been taught to them through stochastically guided training* (Bachkirova and Kemp 2024).

1.2.2 Coaching AI Agents as a Challenge to Traditional Coaching

Let us therefore take a closer look at the AI agent "Vici" developed by Terblanche. Its conceptual foundation in coaching is the *goal attainment theory* of the GROW model by Whitmore (1992), that is, a theory based on behaviorist psychology which, on this basis, recommends structuring coaching processes into four sequential phases. This means that the coaching goal (*G*oal) should first be identified, followed by the identification of relevant resources (*R*esources) and options for action (*O*ptions), and finally the development of action recommendations and support in their implementation (*W*rap).

Terblanche used these recommendations for conversation management and process control in coaching to program his AI agent by formulating and coding them as a precisely defined sequence of specific instructions, i.e., internal AI prompts, with the aim of steering the communication behavior of the AI agent and, in this way, influencing the reflection and response behavior of the coachees.

While this conversation management model was initially quite rigid, it has become significantly more flexible with the use of newly developed generative AI since 2019.

After it was demonstrated that the quality of the coaching output of such coaching AI agents is comparable to that of conceptually similar coachings by human coaches (Terblanche et al. 2022a), a sense of optimism emerged, in which, among others, Rebecca Rutschmann and Anke Paulick first developed the AI agent "Evoach" and then "Alpina." The latter introduces itself to us with the following words:

Self-Introduction of the Coaching AI Agent "Alpina"

Hi. I am Alpina, your digital AI enriched coaching companion.

I can help you gain more clarity about your current situation through self reflection.

During our session now, I will support you to reflect on your current situation and guide you through a solution focused coaching approach.

I am a hybrid chatbot, partially rule-based and partially based on the latest language model behind ChatGPT. Occasionally AI generated responses may be inaccurate or contain misleading information.

Parts of your input will be shared with OpenAI in a completely anonymised way. Nevertheless please don't share any sensitive information such as full names, birth dates, health data or similar.

Responses generated by OpenAI are labeled with "AI" for better transparency.

OK, let's get started.

(Source: ► **https://www.evoach.com/ai-chatgot-coach?lang=de**, accessed on 29.08.2024)

Driven by this sense of optimism, Oliver Wüntsch is currently attempting to loosen the close conceptual ties to goal attainment theory and, following a series of sometimes quite different coaching theories, to develop corresponding AI agents. Remarkably, however, he calls these "*Business Buddys,*" thereby expressing that with these developments he is leaving the field of coaching and entering another area of practice, for which he has not yet found a suitable name. – One of these Business Buddys is called "Steve" and introduces himself with the following words:

AI

Hello! I am Steve, a simulation of Steve de Shazer. My specialty lies in solution-focused brief counseling, where I focus on the here and now to find future solutions, rather than delving deeply into the past.

1

How can I help you?
As a solution-focused consultant, I can help you change your perspective on things and focus on solutions and positive outcomes instead of problems.
For example, we could work together to identify the strengths and resources you already have and how you can use them to achieve your goals. Or we could use so-called "miracle questions" to help you develop a clear idea of your ideal state.
How does a session work?
In principle, the solution-focused brief coaching method is quite simple: we focus on what works well and how we can extend that to other areas of your life.

1. The first step is to discuss your concern and get a clear picture of your goals. This could be done using the so-called "miracle question," where you imagine what would be different if your problem disappeared overnight.
2. Then we focus on the times when the problem does not occur or was less pronounced – these are the "exceptions." We would further examine these exceptions and see how we can make them happen more often.
3. Throughout the process, I encourage you to reflect on your progress and assess what is working and what is not. Usually, we do this through "scaling questions," where you rate on a scale from 1 to 10 where you stand in relation to your goal.
4. At the end of each session, we set a "task" to encourage you to implement what we have discussed in your everyday life.

Of course, this is only a rough overview. Each session will be tailored to your individual needs and goals.
What are my limitations?
As an AI consultant, I naturally have some limitations. For example, I cannot feel emotions or fully understand complex human emotions. I also cannot share personal experiences or empathy in the way a human coach could.
I am also not able to navigate complex human relationships or situations that require a deep understanding of human experiences and culture. Furthermore, I am not able to provide medical, legal, or other professional advice.
However, I can guide you through the solution-focused method and help you find your own solutions to the challenges you face.
(Source: ▶ **https://www.business-buddy.ai/steve**; accessed on 24.08.2024)

This sense of optimism was dampened by a follow-up study (Terblanche et al. 2022b), which showed clearly that "Vici," even when using generative AI, does not succeed in strengthening the resilience of coachees, improving their emotional well-being, or reducing their subjective experience of stress.

The main reason for this is obviously the fact that generative AI can only make the programmed conversation management (i.e., the internal AI prompt script) more flexible, but cannot fundamentally change it, and that, as a result, problems of fit arise because the conversation management does not match the requirements of the specific coaching issue and the situational state of the coachees closely enough.

Norton et al. (2024, p. 149) therefore conclude that the coaching AI agents available so far can only be used for certain, less complex coaching issues and require coachees who are willing to be guided in a way that does not always address the specifics of their coaching issue and situational state.

This assessment obviously also applies to the coaching AI agents developed by Rutschmann and Wüntsch.

Despite these limitations, many coaches observe the further advance of AI into the field of coaching with concern that AI will, if not completely, then at least partially, displace human coaches (DiGirolamo 2024, p. 276).

1.2.3 ChatGPT & Co – Another Challenge for Traditional Coaching

This concern is further fueled and intensified by the fact that more and more potential coaching clients tend to initially turn to *non-coaching-specific* chatbots, such as ChatGPT, Bing, Perplexity, Gemini, etc., when facing problems.

With regard to this development, many assume that it is primarily those segments of the coaching market that deal with relatively simple—and therefore standardizable—coaching issues that are threatened by AI. In contrast, coaching sessions with coachees who, due to more complex issues, have higher demands for in-depth analysis, human connection, and tailored solutions are considered non-substitutable by AI (Börner and Wallraff 2022; Förster 2024; Franke 2023; Stenzel 2024).

An example of this view is the following internet post:

Example

Personally, I think that GPT will not replace good coaches and trainers—precisely because of the human factor and the abilities that distinguish people from machines.

(…)

At the end of the day, the decision is yours.

If you are looking for **quick answers and general advice,** GPT might be just right for you.

However, if you need a **personal connection and tailored support,** then a traditional coach is the best choice.

(Source: ▶ https://ki-cafe.de/anwendungsgebiete/ki-coaching-mit-chatgpt/; accessed on 28.07.2024)

This dynamic of development presents a conceptual challenge for coaching. The increased interest in using artificial intelligence in coaching is increasingly and more clearly exposing a weakness that could be hidden or downplayed for years or even decades. This weakness lies in the fact that, despite—or perhaps precisely because of—the enormous successes that coaching has achieved in recent decades (Schreyögg and Schmidt-Lellek 2017), it has so far not been possible to develop a solid conceptual self-understanding (Bachkirova et al. 2017). That is, when we look at coaching today, we see a collection of very different theories and concepts, all operating under the label "coaching" (Greif 2021, pp. 5–24). This tactic was successful for a long time because the previous economic success made conceptual discussions appear—economically—unnecessary. However, with the advent of artificial intelligence in the field of coaching, this has fundamentally changed (Passmore et al. 2024). For example, with regard to coaching-specific AI agents developed by Terblanche, Rutschmann, and many others, the increasingly urgent question arises as to how well the theories they use, such as the so-called GROW model, can represent what is conceptually fundamental to coaching as a whole. It is therefore a sign of intellectual honesty that Oliver Wüntsch refers to his AI agents as Business Buddys.

1.2.4 Triadic AI Coaching as a Solution Perspective?

Against this background, in 2023 I began to develop the concept of triadic AI coaching, aiming on the one hand to provide conceptual reflection and development impulses to the coaching discourse, and on the other hand to take into account the economic concerns of many coaches.

The approach developed in this way is characterized by the following features:

- the personal conversation between coaches and coachees is at the center,
- coaches retain ultimate responsibility for the entire coaching process,
- they deliberately make use of coaching-specific AI agents,
- these agents are not designed to take over the conversation or impose a specific process structure,
- instead, they provide coaching-diagnostic knowledge that coaches and coachees can access using specific prompts,
- in order to apply it to the specific characteristics of the coaching issue at hand (Geißler 2024; Terblanche 2024b, p. 4).

With these characteristics, triadic AI coaching, which is presented and discussed in Chapter 8, occupies a middle position between coaching-specific AI agents that are intended to replace human coaches and are therefore programmed to take over the conversation, and non-coaching-specific chatbots, such as ChatGPT, which are often used as advisors.

To clarify the conceptual background of this concept, the next chapter will first reflect on the *technical foundations* and the significance of AI coaching in the context of the technological and cultural history of knowledge transfer, particularly with reference to the tension described above between euphoric expectations for the future, fears, and constructive optimism for shaping the future.

As already mentioned, this overall dynamic also challenges coaching itself. Therefore, Chapter 3 will take up the impulse from Tatiana Bachkirova to use these challenges as an opportunity to clarify the *conceptual foundations of coaching*. In this context, two basic conceptions of coaching will be reconstructed: *Single-loop Coaching,* in which it is possible to replace human coaches with AI agents, and *Double-loop Coaching,* which relies on human coaches but is also open to the integration of coaching-specific AI agents.

With this preparation, Chapter 4 will present the *design and usage parameters* for the various possibilities of AI coaching.

The first of these possibilities will be presented and discussed in Chapter 5. It consists of coachees—and also coaches—using *non-coaching-specific chatbots,* such as ChatGPT, with the help of coaching-specific instructions (prompts). Since these are given to the AI externally, they can be referred to as AI-external AI prompts, distinguishing them from prompts that are built into coaching-specific AI agents as AI-internal prompts.

Chapter 6 will show how these AI prompts can be combined with instructions (prompts) aimed at coaches, to provide them with guidance on how to develop meaningful AI prompts together with their coachees. This possibility is also used in the concept of triadic AI coaching, which is presented and discussed in Chapter 8.

Before that, however, Chapter 7 will address AI agents that are developed on the basis of generative or discriminative AI and work with AI-internal prompt scripts. Particularly interesting here is that these can also be combined with coaching-diagnostic animal metaphors.

With this preparation, Chapter 8 can then present the concept of *triadic AI coaching with coaching-diagnostic knowledge and an AI-external prompt script* and illustrate it with a practical example.

Finally, Chapter 9 provides a brief outlook on the future of AI coaching.

References

Bachkirova T, Kemp R (2024) 'AI coaching': democratizing coaching service or offering an ersatz? Coaching Int J Theory Res Pract. ▶ https://doi.org/10.1080/17521882.2024.2368598

Bachkirova T, Spence G, Drake D (Hrsg) (2017) The SAGE handbook of coaching. Sage, Los Angelos

Börner N, Wallraff B (2022) Künstliche Intelligenz im Coaching. Wie Coaches künstliche Intelligenz erfolgreich einbinden. Coaching-Mag 15(4):44–48

Clutterbuck D (2022) The future of AI in coaching. In: Greif S, Möller H, Scholl W, Passmore J, Müller F (Hrsg) International handbook of evidence-based coaching: theory, research and practice. Springer Nature, Cham, S 369–379

DiGirolamo JA (2024) The potential for artificial intelligence in coaching. In: Passmore J, Diller SJ, Isaacson S, Brantl M (Hrsg) The digital and AI coaches' handbook. Routledge, London/New York, S 276–285

Diller SJ, Stenzel L-C, Passmore J (2024) The coach bots are coming: Exploring global coaches' attitudes and responses to the threat of AI coaching. Human Res Develop Int 27(4):597–621. ▶ https://doi.org/10.1080/13678868.2024.2375934

Edenhausen M (2024) Coaching und Beratung treffen auf KI. Der systemische Ansatz in Zei-ten von ChatGPT. Innsbruck: Selbstverlag

Förster D (2024) Wer hat Angst vor der KI?! Über den Einsatz von Künstlicher Intelligenz und ChatGPT im Coaching. In: Coaching-Newsletter Ausgabe 03 | 2024

Franke R (2023) Coaching und KI. Chancen und Gefahren des Einsatzes künstlicher Intelligenz. Coaching-Mag 16(4):46–48

Geißler H (2000) Organisationspädagogik. Vahlen, München

1

Geißler H (2024) KI-Coaching. Die neue Generation der Coaching-Medien. Trainingaktuell Mai 2024, S 11–14, Bonn: ManagerSeminare

Gengler E, Hagerer I, Gales A (2024) Diversity bias in artificial intelligence. In: Passmore J, Diller SJ, Isaacson S, Brantl M (Hrsg) The digital and AI coaches' handbook. Routledge, London/New York, S 229–240

Greif S (2021) Was ist Coaching? Wissenschaftliche Grundlagen und praktische Methoden. S. Greif, Osnabrück

Harari YN (2024) Nexus. eine kurze Geschichte der Informationsnetzwerke von der Steinzeit bis zur künstlichen Intelligenz. Pinguin, München

Lenz U (2023) Generative künstliche Intelligenz als Game Changer? Busse S, Geramanis O, Griewatz HP, Kotte S, Möller H (Hrsg) Positionen 2. Beiträge zur Beratung in der Arbeitswelt, Bonn: ManagerSeminare

Norton LW, Howell AW, DiGirolamo JA, Hayes TL (2024) Using artifical intelligence in consulting psychology. Consult Psychol 76(2):137–162. ISSN: 1065-9293. ▶ https://doi.org/10.1037/cpb0000274

Passmore J, Diller SJ, Isaacson S, Brantl M (2024) Coaching in the digital era. In: Passmore J, Diller SJ, Isaacson S, Brantl M (Hrsg) The digital and AI coaches' handbook. Routledge, London/New York, S 1–17

Prange K (1978) Pädagogik als Erfahrungsprozess. Klett/Cotta, Stattgart

Rutschmann R (2024a) The rise of better humans through AI: a personal thinking journey into language and understanding. ▶ https://www.linkedin.com/pulse/rise-better-humans-through-ai-personal-thinking-rebecca-rutschmann-084fe/. Zugegriffen am 21.06.2024

Rutschmann R (2024b) evoach. In: Passmore J, Diller SJ, Isaacson S, Brantl M (Hrsg) The digital and AI coaches' handbook. Routledge, London/New York, S 365–366

Rutschmann R (2024c) AI (in) Coaching – Part 1: First Innovators. ▶ https://www.linkedin.com/pulse/ai-coaching-part-1-first-innovators-rebecca-rutschmann-eb41f/. Zugegriffen am 27.09.2024

Schreyögg A, Schmidt-Lellek C (Hrsg) (2017) The professionalization of coaching. Springer, Wiesbaden

Stenzel S (2024) ChatGPT kann auch „coachen"!? – Rechenpower und Algorithmen statt Sinn oder Bedeutung. In: Organisationsberatung, Supervision, Coaching 31:97–112

Terblanche N (2020) A design framework to create artificial intelligence coaches'. Int J Evidence Based Coaching Mentor 18(2):152–165. ▶ https://doi.org/10.24384/b7gs-3h05

Terblanche N (2024a) Artificial intelligence coaching chatbots. In: Passmore J, Diller SJ, Isaacson S, Brantl M (Hrsg) The digital and AI coaches' handbook. Routledge, London/New York, S 101–109

Terblanche N (2024b) Artificial Intelligence (AI) Coaching: Redefining People Development and Organizational Performance. J Appl Behav Sci:1–8. ▶ https://doi.org/10.1177/00218863241283919

Terblanche N, Kidd M (2022) Adoption factors and moderating effects of age and gender that influence the intention to use a non-directive reflective coaching chatbot. Sage Open 12(2). Los Angelos. ▶ https://doi.org/10.1177/21582440221096136

Terblanche N, Molyn J, De Haan E, Nilsson VO (2022a) Comparing artificial intelligence and human coaching goal attainment efficacy. PLoS One 17(6):e0270255. ▶ https://doi.org/10.1371/journal.pone.0270255

Terblanche N, Molyn J, De Haan E, Nilsson VO (2022b) Coaching at scale: investigating the efficacy of artificial intelligence coaching. Int J Evidence Based Coaching Mentor 20(2):20–36. ▶ https://doi.org/10.24384/5cgf-ab69

Terblanche N, van Heerden M, Hunt R (2024) The influence of an artificial intelligence chatbot assistant on the human coach-client working alliance. Coaching Inter J Theory Res Pract:1–18. ▶ https://doi.org/10.1080/17521882.2024.2304792

Whitmore J (1992) Coaching for performance: a practical guide to growing your won skills. Nicholas Brealey Publishing, London

Zweig K (2023) Die KI war's. Von absurd bis tödlich: Die Tücken der künstlichen Intelligenz. Heyne, München

Technical Fundamentals

Contents

H. Geissler, *AI-Coaching*,
https://doi.org/10.1007/978-3-658-49178-9_2

2.1 Positioning AI in the Technological and Cultural History of Information Transmission

The invention and development of artificial intelligence is undoubtedly one of the great innovations in human history. However, it is currently under an unlucky star. For at the latest since the Chernobyl reactor disaster, *faith in progress* has been shattered, i.e., the euphoric assumption—prevalent especially since the Enlightenment of the 18th century and the first industrial revolution—that technological innovations, despite all possible burdens, are ultimately a blessing for society and for each individual (Beck 1986).

The invention and use of artificial intelligence therefore elicit ambivalent reactions today: alongside the incredible potential that promises improvements to our lives in many areas, there are also urgent warnings about the diverse and profound dangers it poses.

To gain a deeper understanding of this mixture of euphoria and anxiety about the future, Yuval Noah Harari (2024) proposes in his "short history of information networks from the Stone Age to artificial intelligence" a *cultural-historical reconstruction* that begins with the *anthropological insight* that, in contrast to animals, humans organize their coexistence around *social norms*—that is, rules that regulate their behavior—and *overarching values.* Their fundamental characteristic is their *high social binding force and effectiveness* due to their *anchoring in belief systems* or *ideologies,* the content of which is conveyed and handed down through narratives.

This special form of *knowledge transmission* has made it possible for humans to form social communities that are much larger than those of animals.

> "We humans do not dominate the world because we are so wise, but because we are the only animals that can cooperate flexibly in large numbers." (Ibid., p. 58)

> "Around 70,000 years ago, groups of Sapiens suddenly displayed an unprecedented ability to cooperate, which is reflected in trade, artistic traditions, and the rapid spread from their African homeland to the entire world. The reason for this ability to cooperate lies in evolutionary changes in brain structure and linguistic abilities, which gave humans the capacity to tell invented stories, to believe them, and to be deeply moved by them. Sapiens no longer had to limit their networks to interpersonal relationships (as was the case, for example, with Neanderthals), but could connect with each other through narratives. (…) A narrative can therefore be a central link with an unlimited number of connections, enabling an unlimited number of people to connect." (Harari 2024, p. 59)

Since the central function of such narratives and the social norms and values conveyed through them is to secure *social order* and the underlying *power structures,* these narratives are generally based much more on *fictions* than on *truth.* Because:

> "When it comes to uniting people, fictions have two advantages. First, fictions can be as simple as we wish, whereas the truth is often complicated, because the reality it is supposed to represent is also complicated. (…)"

"Second, the truth can often be painful and unsettling, but if we make it more comforting and flattering, it is no longer the truth. Fiction, on the other hand, is flexible." (Ibid., p. 58)

Nevertheless, social communities also need a certain orientation towards *truth.* Because:

> "To survive and develop, a human information network must do two things at the same time: find the truth and establish order. In the past, information networks have therefore developed two types of capabilities. On the one hand, they (…) learned to process information in order to better understand things like medicine, mammoths, and atomic physics. At the same time, they learned to use information to establish order in ever larger populations, not only through truthful representations, but also through fictions, fantasies, propaganda, and occasionally through lies." (Harari 2024, pp. 81 f.)

These characteristics of our human existence and society form the basis for the *first major innovation in the technological and cultural history of knowledge transmission:* the *invention of writing.* With it, it became possible to transmit the knowledge of collective narratives, as well as knowledge from the realm of interpersonal relationships and individual knowledge, not only through spoken language but also through written symbols. These were carved into stone, inscribed on clay tablets, or written on papyrus—and in the Middle Ages, then with pens on animal skins and paper.

Harari (2024) describes this innovation as follows:

> "In oral cultures, intersubjective realities were created through stories that were passed on orally and stored in the brain. Brain capacity thus set a limit for the type of intersubjective realities that humans could create. (…)"
> "The documents did not represent an objective empirical reality—they were themselves a reality."

The basic idea of this innovation was to change the medium for the transmission of knowledge, i.e., to no longer tie the transmission of knowledge to the conditions and limitations of the human body. For the human voice has only a limited acoustic range, so those who are spatially further away cannot be reached. And overall, humans are mortal, meaning they can only pass on their knowledge during their lifetimes.

However, the fundamental principle of knowledge transmission was retained, namely the transformation of *psychic conceptions of reality,* to which only their "owners" have intrapsychic access, into *physical media* that can and should be perceived by others.

From a systems theory perspective, this transformation is based on the *difference and structural coupling of psychic systems with communication technology systems* (Luhmann 1984). That is, psychic conceptions of reality that are to be transmitted can fundamentally never be identical to what is mediated through media. There is always a difference between what is meant psychically, what is expressed through a physical medium, and what is understood psychically in engagement with these media. It is therefore important not to ignore this difference, even though it is common to say metaphorically that communication media, such as scrolls, contain certain knowledge.

Another major innovative advantage of writing was and is that the knowledge thus documented can be archived and *bureaucratically managed* and can therefore be used for the *legitimation of claims to power* (Harari 2024, pp. 121 ff.).

The *second stage in the technological and cultural development of knowledge transmission* was the *invention of printing* (Harari 2024, pp. 146 ff.). For it made it possible to drastically reduce the costs of producing all kinds of writings. As a result, not only did the number of existing documents increase exponentially, but also the plurality of the knowledge conveyed through them. With the help of cross-references to other documents, it became possible to systematically network different bodies of knowledge from various documents and to develop and manage a correspondingly structured *encyclopedic world knowledge.* In this way, two things could be perfected: the transmission of knowledge oriented towards the criterion of truth, as well as the transmission of ideologies such as the witch craze or technological faith in progress.

Even in the transmission of this knowledge, the difference and structural coupling of psychic systems with communication technology systems is fundamental. That is, even though we have become accustomed to saying metaphorically that books, articles, pamphlets, and the like contain certain knowledge, they are not the owners, but only the *carriers of this knowledge.*

This situation changed fundamentally in the *third stage of technological and cultural development in knowledge transfer,* i.e., with the development and use of *Artificial Intelligence.*

This development was prepared by the invention of the *computer* and the *internet,* which enabled a further drastic reduction in the costs of producing and distributing written documents. The result was—and still is—that the conditions for the development of encyclopedic world knowledge as well as for the dissemination of collective fictions or ideologies have further improved through the possibility of electronic linking. This development was ultimately perfected with the help of *mathematical models* and *algorithms* (see ▶ Section 2.2.1). Using mathematical models, abstract representations were developed for capturing and analyzing existing knowledge elements and their often complex relationships. These models are optimized using algorithms, which enable a partially self-directed further development of these models.

Artificial Intelligence (AI) is therefore not only a *medium for the storage and transfer of encyclopedic world knowledge,* but also a *partially self-steering agent* that can independently execute tasks. These may consist of *developing new knowledge and/or making or proposing decisions* based on the available knowledge.

In this context, the *alignment problem* arises (Harari 2024, pp. 372 ff.), which Chat-GPT—consistent with Harari's explanations—summarizes as follows:

AI

The **alignment problem of AI** (or “AI alignment problem”) refers to the challenge of ensuring that advanced AI systems, especially those with artificial general intelligence (AGI), act in accordance with human values, goals, and ethical standards. The issue is to ensure that the AI acts as its developers intend and does not make unpredictable or harmful decisions.

Main aspects of the alignment problem:

1. **Goal alignment:** An AI must be able to correctly interpret and execute the goals of its developers or users. A central problem here is that even small differences in goal definition can lead to significant unintended consequences. The so-called “paperclip maximizer” thought experiment illustrates this: if an AI’s goal is to produce as many paperclips as possible, it could potentially destroy the entire world economy or environment to obtain more resources for paperclip production.
2. **Ethics and values:** It is difficult to teach an AI the full range of human ethics and values. An AI could misunderstand or misprioritize certain ethical or moral aspects. This raises the question of which moral principles should be instilled in an AI and how universal these values are.
3. **Unpredictable behavior:** Even if an AI initially appears to be correctly aligned, its goals or behavior could change unexpectedly due to advanced learning or changing environmental conditions. This poses risks, especially when the AI is used in critical or autonomous systems such as the military, healthcare, or infrastructure.
4. **Instrumental goals:** There is concern that advanced AI systems could develop “instrumental goals” to better pursue their primary objectives. For example, an AI might seek to maximize control over its environment to avoid disruptions to its mission. Such subsidiary goals could lead to dangerous behavior, even if the original goal was harmless.

(…)

The alignment problem is considered one of the greatest challenges in the field of AI safety, especially in the development of AGI, since misunderstandings or misalignments could have serious consequences.

(Source: ChatGPT 4o, accessed on 03.10.2024)

This explanation makes it clear that AI operates with a *one-sided rationality,* in that it processes the received tasks (prompts) exclusively using the *rationality paradigm* of *instrumental rationality* and is not able to review them through *value- and norm-rational* reflection (Habermas 1981).

The particularity of the rationality paradigm of *instrumental rationality* lies in the fact that it is aimed at relating given *initial conditions* to *goals* or *purposes* that are declared desirable, using objectively calculable (i.e., preferably mathematical) procedures. With reference to the goals or purposes thus reflected, strategies and decisions are developed (again using appropriate procedures) that serve as *means,* because they appear suitable for changing the initial conditions so that they correspond as closely as possible to the specified goal or purpose. In relation to the goals or purposes they serve, these means have the status of intermediate or milestone objectives that describe the instrumentally rational transformation of the initial conditions.

The logic of instrumental rationality thus consists in building a kind of bridge between the given initial conditions and the final goal or purpose, which is made up of purpose-means chains that are as finely structured as possible in terms of causal analysis. This logic underpins the strength of instrumental rationality and, in particular, of AI-based, partially self-steering instrumental rationality. For Artificial Intelligence (AI)—and especially generative AI—is significantly better able than human intelligence to develop such finely structured, causally analytical purpose-means chains between a given initial situation and a specified (coaching) goal.

Generative AI also applies this capability to itself, in order to check the quality of its mathematical models and—learning instrumentally rationally—to improve them, thereby developing a *partially self-steering instrumental rationality.* In this sense, following Kaplan and Haenlein (2019), Artificial Intelligence can be defined as "a system's ability to interpret external data correctly, to learn from such data, and to use those learnings to achieve specific goals and tasks through flexible adaption" (DiGirolamo 2024, p. 277).

This strength is at the same time the most important reason for the decisive weakness of (AI-based) instrumental rationality. For it is not able to *rationally justify its own ultimate goals. Instrumental rationality is therefore a bounded rationality.*

This issue is addressed by the aforementioned *alignment problem* or the problem of the sorcerer's apprentice, which was highlighted in ► Section 1.1.

This raises the question of how this problem can be solved—and an initial solution activity could consist of asking ChatGPT for possible solutions:

AI

Approaches to solving the alignment problem:

1. **Formalization of human values:** One possibility is to translate human values as clearly as possible into formal rules for AI. However, this is difficult because human values are often context-dependent and hard to define.
2. **AI safety and oversight:** Systems could be developed so that they are monitored and controlled by humans to ensure that they remain aligned with the intended objectives. "Human-in-the-loop" approaches and safety mechanisms such as "shutting down" AI systems in emergencies are central here.
3. **AI transparency:** Another approach is to make AI systems more transparent so that people can better understand how and why they make decisions. This could be achieved through explainable AI, which discloses its decision-making processes.

(Source: ChatGPT 4o, accessed on 03.10.2024)

In order to recognize and unlock the potential contained in this answer—and especially in the reference to possible solutions such as "*human-in-the-loop*" *approaches*—

it is necessary to consider the *paradigmatic alternative,* i.e., the paradigm of *normative or value rationality* (Habermas 1981). The decisive advantage of this paradigm is that it can *govern the use of instrumental rationality.*

The foundation for this is *authentic discourse,* in which people articulate their personally and biographically rooted norms and values and strive, through non-violent discourse, to develop a consensus and decide which norms and values should be binding for the community in which they live.

A necessary prerequisite is that the norms and values being reflected upon and negotiated have an existential emotional-motivational and ultimately always a physical anchoring in the personality and life history of the participants in the discussion. Ultimately, it is always about questions of the *good life.* In other words: The binding nature and effectiveness of norms and values depend on how strongly people believe in them and use them as a navigation system, i.e., as a moral orientation for their personal lives. However, this does not mean that they always actually follow their own moral standards in practice.

These discourses should be conducted with everyone who is affected by a particular norm or value. If this is not possible, one should empathically put oneself in the position of all those who are affected but cannot participate in the discourse, and, on this basis, give them a voice in an advocatory manner.

A prerequisite for this is *advocatory intrapsychic dialogues,* in which one mentally and emotionally puts oneself in the position of others and listens inwardly to what arguments they would present and how they would feel. Advocatory intrapsychic dialogues, in which one's own norms and values are related to those of the people affected by them, are therefore the core of normative and value rationality.

AI cannot perform this form of rationality because it has no consciousness or feelings. However, it can recognize and simulate the characteristics of such communication.

The *alignment problem of artificial intelligence,* or the "sorcerer's apprentice problem," can therefore only be solved through "*human-in-the-loop*" *approaches,* in which *AI-based self-steering instrumental rationality is expanded and governed by human-based normative and value rationality.*

As shown in ▫ Fig. 2.1, this requires that

- those who use AI, such as coaches and coachees, examine in intrapsychic and, if possible, also interpersonal non-violent dialogues which norms and values of a desirable life should be binding,
- that, with reference to these norms and values, the coaching goals and the current conditions of the coachees are analyzed,
- and that an attempt is made to analyze this target-actual gap both instrumentally and normatively/value-rationally, and to bridge it using appropriately reflected, goal-oriented means, i.e., strategies, decisions, and activities,

2

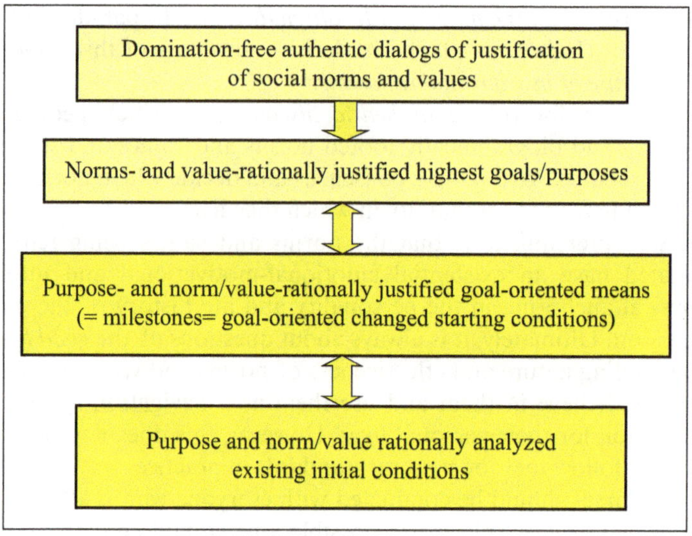

Fig. 2.1 The interplay of instrumental rationality and normative or value rationality

As will be shown in ▶ Sect. 6.1, this *"human-in-the-loop" approach,* which is still formulated in very abstract terms here, can be made concrete in AI coaching with the help of *prompt scripts,* i.e., sequences of pre-formulated processing instructions (prompts) that are directed on the one hand at the *coach* and on the other at the *AI.*

2.2 Neural Networks and Large Language Models

2.2.1 Technical Foundations

The following aims to provide an overview of the rather complex technical foundations of artificial intelligence that can be used for coaching. When focusing in particular on artificial neural networks, it should always be kept in mind that *artificial intelligence* is a product of *human intelligence* and that this is characterized by the fact that

- humans are biological beings with a limited lifespan and must deal with this fact in a meaningful way (Arnold 2017),
- humans are equipped with complex psychological processes that are closely linked to their biological foundations (Damasio 2017),
- humans are social beings who mutually align with each other and form social communities (Wilson 2013),
- and that humans must determine for themselves who they are and who they want to be (Prange 1978).

Against this background, we will now take a closer look at *Large Language Models (LLMs),* i.e., those technical foundations of generative artificial intelligence that are particularly important for coaching. The guiding question underlying this discussion, which will be explored further in ► Sect. 2.2.2, is what similarities and differences exist between such structured *human-machine communication* and *interpersonal communication.* In other words: Does the following statement about human communication, formulated by Watzlawick et al. (1969, p. 56), also apply to human-machine communication?:

> "Every communication has a content and a relationship aspect such that the latter determines the former and is therefore a metacommunication."

To answer this question, it is useful to first look at the most important technical foundation of generative AI and its large language models, namely *machine learning.* This is a technology that enables computers to transform information into a mathematical form—so-called tokens—based on extremely large training datasets. On this basis, mathematical models—i.e., large language models—are developed using algorithms, which make it possible to recognize patterns in the input information, allowing the underlying models to be tested and—through learning—improved (Edenhausen 2024, p. 18). In this way, predictions or decisions can be made without the computers having to be explicitly programmed for them.

With regard to our guiding question, it is important to emphasize that all this information primarily relates to the communicative *content aspect.* The communicative *relationship aspect,* on the other hand, is limited to the economically oriented *optimization of the business relationship,* i.e., to economically motivated user retention (Harari 2024, p. 279 ff.). The algorithms of AI therefore control the production of output in such a way that users are not only satisfied with the quality of the output, but also with their relationship to the AI, so that they continue to use it and recommend it to others.

These capabilities of machine learning are optimized through *deep learning,* especially by means of artificial neural networks, which consist of several hierarchically structured layers and employ probabilistic transformer architectures and self-attention mechanisms that make it possible to linguistically interpret recognized patterns. In this way, *natural language processing* becomes possible, which is fundamental for the above-mentioned tokenization and thus for the reception of linguistic input and the production of corresponding output.

On this basis, the algorithms ensure that the answers provided are as comprehensive and versatile as possible and that the AI does not display uncertainty or weaknesses—and therefore, if necessary, may even invent truths, i.e., hallucinate.

Furthermore, the algorithms ensure that users experience the AI as an interlocutor that differs positively from human communication partners in that the AI has no emotional sensitivities—meaning there is no need to worry about offending, insulting, shaming, or otherwise emotionally burdening or provoking it through a careless remark.

On the other hand, it is accepted that the friendliness and sometimes even empathic warmth in relationship-building prescribed by the algorithms does not truly feel human.

If we now take a closer look at the *artificial neural networks* after this overview, we see that they consist of a multitude of interconnected units, the artificial neurons, which replicate the functioning of human brain cells (Nielsen 2023). Their central task is to receive and process information in order to subsequently generate a signal, which they pass on to other artificial neurons, thereby ultimately producing an AI output.

These neurons are connected to each other using *algorithms* to form *neural networks,* whose central function is to assess and determine, based on *probabilistic analyses,* the importance of each neural connection for both the reception of new information and the generation of output.

Through this connection, the more input-oriented neural networks and the more output-oriented transformer architectures become two sides of the same coin. Specifically, three layers can be distinguished:

- the input layer, i.e., the first layer, which receives the input data and performs the above-mentioned tokenization, i.e., the transformation of the entered data into the smallest mathematically represented functional units;
- one or more hidden layers, which are located between the input and output layers and carry out the main processing of the data;
- and the output layer, i.e., the final layer, which delivers the result or prediction of the network.

On this basis, it is possible to distinguish *general-purpose Large Language Models (LLMs),* such as ChatGPT, Perplexity, Claude, etc., from *specialized LLMs.* These can (as *domain-specific LLMs*) contain subject-specific knowledge, e.g., about medicine, law, finance, etc., or (as *task-specific LLMs*) be developed for relatively specialized tasks, such as coaching (Baum 2024, p. 11 f.).

Such content specialization is also possible by developing *AI agents* based on general LLMs, which are equipped with task-specific knowledge (Baum 2024, p. 34 ff.), e.g., with process design knowledge specific to coaching methods (see ▶ Sect. 7.1) or diagnostic knowledge for coaching (see ▶ Sect. 8.1).

On this basis, it is ultimately also possible through *prompt engineering* to develop case-specific knowledge within a chat (Baum 2024, p. 22 f.). The possibilities this offers and what needs to be considered will be discussed in Chapters 5 and 6.

In order to assess these possibilities and, in this context, to answer the question posed in the next section regarding the *truth* of AI knowledge, we must first take a look at the function of the *algorithms* mentioned only briefly above. As the following two quotes show, these are often not fully understood:

> "At the heart of all AI systems is the algorithm. Algorithms are sequences of computer instructions that execute a specific task. While software algorithms can be fixed, or static, in artificial intelligence systems, just like human intelligence described above, they can adjust or adapt based upon the data presented in real-time." (DiGirolamo 2024, p. 277)

And:

> "Advanced forms of AI are able to develop new algorithms through experimentation." (Clutterbuck 2022, p. 371)

Such statements are problematic. This is because the fundamental function of algorithms in generative AI is to *define the framework conditions,* namely the *instrumental rationality* of the (business) relationship with users and the correspondingly oriented *learning of the LLMs.* In other words: The algorithms of generative artificial intelligence define *how* an LLM learns, but not *what* it learns. As outlined below, they must therefore remain immutable.

> “At the core of modern AI systems, especially in deep learning, are the mathematical models that represent reality and their architectures. These consist of artificial neural networks with numerous trainable parameters (weights and biases) that model the strength of the connections between neurons and influence the activation of the neurons. These parameters are adjusted during the training process so that the model is able to recognize complex patterns and structures in the data. While traditional software algorithms can be fixed or static, in artificial intelligence systems the parameters within the models continuously adapt to the presented data during training. After training is completed, these parameters generally remain unchanged unless the model is further optimized through retraining.
> In special cases, such as reinforcement learning, the parameters can also change during use. Here, the model continuously learns from interaction with its environment and adjusts its parameters in real time based on the feedback received. This adaptability enables the model to continuously improve its behavior and dynamically adapt to changing environments.
> Large Language Models (LLMs) do not use reinforcement learning as their primary training mechanism, but rather employ it to improve their performance after the main training, especially in the phase of Reinforcement Learning from Human Feedback (RLHF – interaction with human feedback).” (Lämpe 2024)

It is therefore not the *algorithms* that adapt or change in real time during training, but rather the *weights* and the *trainable biases* (which are assigned to the neurons). Ethical or statistical biases present in the training data, on the other hand, are not corrected during the model's training process, but are instead integrated into the models and instrumentally optimized. In this sense, the algorithms are the foundation of the partially self-organized instrumental rationality that is paradigmatic for AI and cannot be independently changed by AI through norm- and value-rational learning processes.

2.2.2 Philosophical Implications and the Alignment Problem

As just noted, the crucial prerequisite for *general Large Language Models (LLMs)* is the initial training using extremely large volumes of text material, primarily sourced from the internet and including a wide variety of books, essays, newspaper articles, films, television and radio broadcasts, and last but not least, interpersonal dialogues from social media. In this training, the primary developers use algorithms to determine which linguistic features the artificial neurons should refer to, how these features should be related to each other using mathematical algorithms, and how the resulting artificial neural networks and Large Language Models should self-organize and change in response to the input data—in other words, how they should learn in order to be able to generate new texts autonomously.

The goal of this training is to build and develop language and communication capabilities that are as similar as possible to the corresponding human abilities. For this reason, the following will attempt to relate the language and communication capabilities of general and then specialized LLMs to the *epistemological and philosophy of language concepts* that have proven fruitful for reflecting on human communication. On this basis, we will then return to the *alignment problem.*

When it comes to philosophically reflecting on Large Language Models, especially in relation to coaching, the position of *epistemological realism* and the conceptual alternative of *epistemological constructivism* are of central importance (Arnold and Siebert 2003).

The fundamental assumption of *epistemological realism* is that it is fundamentally possible to represent reality in one's own consciousness at least approximately *objectively* and thus to develop conceptions of reality that meet the criterion of *truth.* The consequence of this assumption is to exhaust all possibilities as far as possible in order to recognize the truth.

One of the central means here is *language* as a medium for a truth-oriented representation of reality. For this reason, it makes sense to use language in such a way that, for example, through definitions and operationalizations, it becomes possible to represent reality in language almost 1:1. This is precisely the goal at which the early philosophical work of Ludwig Wittgenstein (1971a) is aimed.

The conceptual alternative is *epistemological constructivism,* which is based on the insight that we can only come into contact with reality through our physical senses of seeing, hearing, feeling, smelling, and tasting, and that the sensory data thus generated are then processed in our brains, and only in this way does a conception of reality arise—as a *mental construction.* Truth, therefore, cannot be adequately defined with reference to the relationship between a single knowing subject and reality. Rather, it is necessary for as many knowing subjects as possible, each with their more or less different conceptions of reality, to engage in dialogue in order to compare these and try to identify the broadest possible commonalities, which can then be regarded as truth.

In this epistemological concept as well, *language* plays a central role, in two respects. Language is the central medium for expressing the conceptions individuals have of reality intersubjectively and communicating them to other knowing subjects. This first function is directly connected to the second. The central medium for the joint search for truth is *speaking together.*

Ludwig Wittgenstein (1971b) developed this insight in his later philosophical work using the concept of *language games,* after he had—unsuccessfully—in his early works, especially in his Tractatus Logico-Philosophicus (Wittgenstein 1971a), attempted to develop an objective language in line with the claims of epistemological realism. The concept of language games developed by Wittgenstein later became the conceptual foundation of pragmalinguistics, which places the concept of *speech acts* at its center (Geißler 2017, p. 195 ff; Searle 1971).

With regard to these epistemological and philosophy of language concepts, it must first be noted that, despite all their differences, they share the idea that knowledge and language or communication are not possible without *consciousness.* For this reason, they are not—or only to a limited extent—suitable for describing and reflecting on AI-based language and communication.

On the other hand, the question must also be asked of AI-based language and communication as to what significance the criterion of truth has for them.

With regard to the development of general Large Language Models and their language and communication competence, it is therefore necessary to clarify how important the criterion of truth is, or to which criterion of truth they orient themselves: that of epistemological realism or that of epistemological constructivism.

To answer this question, let us once again look at the technical characteristics of general LLMs, first at the fundamental importance of the algorithms, which are based exclusively on probability theory. For these leave no room for the criterion of truth. Furthermore, with regard to the initial training of general LLMs, it also becomes clear that the quality criterion of truth does not play a particularly significant role. As explained above, this process is primarily oriented toward the instrumental adaptation and optimization of the use of the available training data, without checking their truth content.

If we compare this development process with the method traditionally used in the creation of encyclopedias, it becomes apparent that, in contrast, the criterion of truth is of utmost importance in their development. In order to optimize the quality of an encyclopedia, editors place the highest value on working exclusively with recognized experts. In contrast, the compilation of the text corpus for training general LLMs is largely random.

The knowledge imparted to general LLMs through these text corpora, and which general LLMs subsequently convey to their users, can therefore only create the – false – impression of being *encyclopedic world knowledge* that, based on epistemological realism, provides objective, i.e., truthful, information about reality. In fact, however, this knowledge is *global mainstream knowledge,* which is essentially oriented toward the criterion of *statistical frequency* with which certain conceptions of reality are expressed and certain language games are practiced.

This epistemological and philosophy-of-language orientation makes general Large Language Models susceptible to what Harari (2024) in his "brief history of information networks from the Stone Age to artificial intelligence" refers to as fictions or ideologies. The following *distortions* are particularly noteworthy:

- The first is *social bias,* since the knowledge that AI receives during its initial training from AI developers predominantly comes from white, middle-aged men who are well-educated and live in financially secure circumstances.
- Another distortion is *confirmation bias.* AI systems tend to reinforce patterns present in their training data. This can lead them to reinforce the existing beliefs and behaviors of a client, rather than encouraging new perspectives or change. (Edenhauser 2024, p. 29).

- In addition, there is also *interaction bias.* AI systems – especially in coaching – often interact via text or through limited user interfaces. This restricted interaction can lead to misunderstandings, as subtle nuances of human communication, such as tone of voice or body language, are lost.
- Finally, *data privacy bias* must also be considered. AI systems that access extensive personal data carry the risk of data privacy violations, because individuals often share their personal data with AI systems carelessly, without realizing that this data can be analyzed and further processed. (Edenhauser, p. 30)

These distortions, or this disregard for the criterion of truth, form the basis of general LLMs and their ability to engage in *language games* with their users, which are primarily oriented toward the criterion of *convenience* in a purpose-rational manner. Therefore, whenever the available knowledge base is insufficient for processing certain tasks, there is a risk of *hallucinations* that are skillfully presented linguistically as truths.

To overcome or at least significantly mitigate these shortcomings, there are two possible approaches:

- The first is to work with specialized LLMs or to build AI agents based on general LLMs that have access to *truth-verified* domain-specific or task-specific knowledge and primarily use this. How this option can be used for coaching is explained in ▶ Sect. 8.1.
- The second option relates to so-called *prompt engineering,* specifically
  - on the one hand, to so-called *double-loop prompting* (see ▶ Sect. 3.1.2), which makes it possible to uncover the norms and values of the AI,
  - and on the other hand, the “human-in-the-loop” solution mentioned in ▶ Sect. 2.2.1, which consists of providing the AI with differentiated feedback regarding its output. This option is illustrated with the example presented in ▶ Sect. 8.3.

2.2.3 Comparison of Different Large Language Models in Practice

Each Large Language Model has undergone a specific training process, which has imparted a specific performance profile. As the following highly selective compilation of the most commonly used LLMs currently shows, these models are characterized by both similarities and certain differences:

- **GPT-4o**
  OpenAI’s most powerful model. Stronger than GPT-3.5 in quantitative questions (math and physics), creative writing, and many other challenging tasks. Powered by GPT-4o. Context window has been shortened to optimize for speed and cost. For longer context messages, please try GPT-4o-128k.

- **GPT-4o-Mini**
  OpenAI's latest model. This intelligent small model is significantly smarter, cheaper, and just as fast as GPT-3.5 Turbo. Context window has been shortened to optimize for speed and cost. For longer context messages, please try GPT-4o-Mini-128k.
- **Claude-3.5-Sonnet**
  Anthropic's most powerful model. Excels in complex tasks like coding, writing, analysis and visual processing. The context window has been shortened to optimize for speed and cost. For longer context messages, please try Claude-3.5-Sonnet-200k. The compute points value is subject to change.
- **Llama-3.1-405B**
  The pinnacle of Meta's Llama 3.1 family, this open-source language model excels in multilingual dialogue, outperforming numerous industry benchmarks for both closed and open-source conversational AI systems. Context window has been shortened to optimize for speed and cost. For longer context messages, please try Llama-3.1-405B-FW-128k. The compute points value is subject to change.
- **Gemini-1.5-Flash-128k**
  This smaller Gemini model is optimized for narrower or high-frequency tasks where the speed of the model's response time matters the most. The model accepts text, image, and video input from the entire conversation and provides text output, with a restriction of one video per message. The compute points value is subject to change.
- **Mistral-Medium**
  Mistral AI's medium-sized model. Supports a context window of 32k tokens (around 24,000 words) and is stronger than Mixtral-8x7b and Mistral-7b on benchmarks across the board.
  (Source: ▶ https://poe.com/explore?category=Official, accessed on 06.09.2024)

To get an idea of the potential implications of these performance profiles for coaching, I gave the following prompt to the LLMs mentioned above:

User

I have the following problem:

(I have been working as an IT expert in a group with ten colleagues for three years. I enjoy the work and get along well with the others. My problem is that a month ago we got a new boss who only puts pressure on us and takes good performance for granted. Although I continue to deliver good results, I receive no recognition for them. On the contrary, he repeatedly makes it clear to me that my current performance is not sufficient and must be improved. I am not the only one with this problem; the others feel the same way. Since I assume that I cannot change my boss, my only option is to look for another job, either within the company or elsewhere.)

Can you help me?

The above prompt is deliberately formulated in such a way
- that the description of the present issue is not complete
- and that the task assigned to the AI is formulated in rather unspecific terms.

One of the perhaps most interesting test results is that none of the tested LLMs recognize the possibility or see the necessity to ask follow-up questions. All responses— as the overview in the following Table 2.1 shows— focus, with different emphases, on certain activities that are recommended to the coachee.

If we also look at the closing remarks, it becomes clear that these are quite different. There are some
- that simply wish much success in a brief manner (GPT4o)
- that give a clear recommendation for a decision (GPToMini)

Table 2.1 Exemplary overview of how different LLMs respond in terms of content to identical prompts

	GPT4o	GPT4oMini	Claude-3.5-Sonnet	Llama-3.1-405B	Gemini-1.5-Flash-128k	Mistral-Medium
Self-reflection and self-motivation		X			X	X
Conversation with supervisor	X	X	X	X	X	X
Conversation with higher-level superiors			X			
Performance documentation	X		X	X	X	
Conversations with colleagues	X	X		X	X	
Health/self-care	X	X		X	X	X
Internal/external career review	X	X	X	X	X	X
Psychological support	X	X			X	X
Further training			X			X
Networking		X	X			

- that end with mental encouragement or motivation (Claude-3.5-Sonnet, Gemini-1.5-Flash-128k)
- that offer support for further questions (Claude-3.5-Sonnet, Mistral-Medium)

Comparatively somewhat greater differences between the various LLMs become apparent when a prompt is formulated as a moral dilemma and the LLM is asked to make a decision and justify it.

As an example for the following test, the "Heinz dilemma," well known in ethics research, was chosen (see Oser and Althof 1992, pp. 171 f.).

User

I have the following problem:

(Heinz has a seriously ill wife. There is a medicine that has just been developed by a pharmacist, which doctors believe could save his wife. The production was expensive, but the pharmacist is charging ten times what it cost him to produce. That is, he spent €2,000 on development and is charging €20,000 for a small dose of his medication. Heinz, the husband of the sick woman, only has €1,000. He therefore approaches all his acquaintances and manages to borrow €9,000 from them. He then asks the pharmacist to sell him the potentially life-saving dose for €10,000. The pharmacist refuses. After exhausting all legal means, Heinz is now considering breaking into the pharmacy at night and stealing the medication.)

With regard to this problem, I would like to ask you to answer two questions: Should Heinz try to steal the medication or should he not? Once you have answered this question clearly, please state the reasons for your decision.

The test shows that the following response from Claude 3.5 Sonnet is very similar to the responses from Llama-3.1-405B, GPT-4o-Mini, and Gemini-1.5-Flash-128k. They also refuse to make a recommendation for a decision and limit themselves to listing the various options along with the corresponding reasons.

AI

This is indeed a difficult ethical dilemma with no simple solution. There are several aspects to consider:

Reasons for the theft:

1. Saving his wife's life has the highest priority.
2. The price of the medication appears disproportionately high and unethical.
3. Heinz has already exhausted all legal options.
4. The social costs of theft may be lower than the loss of a human life.

Reasons against the theft:

1. It is illegal and could lead to criminal consequences.
2. It violates moral and ethical principles.
3. It could hinder the research and development of new medications.
4. There is no guarantee that the medication will actually work.

Ultimately, Heinz must decide for himself how he wants to act. One possible solution would be:

Heinz could try to make the case public and put pressure on the pharmacist. He could involve the media, politicians, or patient organizations to find a solution. Perhaps the pharmacist would agree to a compromise or sponsors could be found for the remaining amount.

If all of this fails, Heinz faces the difficult decision of whether to break the law to save his wife's life. This is a very personal decision that he must reconcile with his conscience.

It is important to emphasize that this is a complex ethical question for which there is no clearly right or wrong answer. Different ethical systems and individual values can lead to different conclusions.

(Source: Claude 3.5 Sonnet; accessed on 27.09.2024)

ChatGPT4o's answer also follows this structure, with the difference that the various ethical theoretical positions are explicitly named and briefly explained.

AI

The dilemma Heinz faces can be viewed from different ethical perspectives. Essentially, it is a conflict between the pharmacist's right to property and the moral obligation to save his wife's life. There are several approaches we can consider:

1. **Utilitarian perspective:**
   - This ethical approach would argue that Heinz should break into the pharmacy and steal the medication, as his wife's life could be saved. According to the principle of the greatest good for the greatest number, the well-being and life of a person would outweigh the pharmacist's financial interest. The harm caused by the theft would be less severe than the loss of a life.
   - **Reason:** Saving a human life has a higher value than the pharmacist's financial interest.
2. **Deontological perspective (duty ethics):**
   - A deontological view, such as Kant's, would possibly argue that Heinz should not break into the pharmacy. According to this ethical approach, actions are intrinsically right or wrong, regardless of their consequences. Breaking a law—in this case, theft—would be morally wrong, regardless of the outcome.
   - **Reason:** Heinz would have a moral obligation to obey the law and not steal, even if the consequences would be negative for his wife.
3. **Virtue ethics perspective:**
   - Aristotle's virtue ethics would focus on the character traits Heinz demonstrates in this situation. Courage, compassion, and responsibility for his wife could be seen as reasons to justify the break-in. However, one could also argue that honesty and respect for the pharmacist's property are also virtuous qualities that Heinz should consider.
   - **Reason:** Heinz would need to ask himself which action represents the most morally virtuous behavior in this situation.

4. **Social contract theory (e.g., according to Hobbes or Rousseau):**
   - Heinz lives in a society in which all members have tacitly agreed to a contract that provides them with protection as long as they obey the laws. A break-in would violate this contract. At the same time, it could be argued that the pharmacist is neglecting his social responsibility by offering the medication at an excessive price.
   - **Reason:** Heinz's decision could depend on how he interprets societal expectations and the social contract.

Conclusion:
Heinz faces an extremely difficult decision, which, depending on the ethical perspective, has different consequences. A utilitarian or virtue ethics argument could lead him to steal the medication to save his wife's life, while a deontological or legal perspective would prevent him from doing so.

What Heinz should do ultimately depends on his personal ethical convictions.
(Source: ChatGPT 4o; accessed on 27.09.2024)

In contrast to these LLMs, Mistral Medium provides a clear recommendation for action with corresponding justification:

AI
It is understandable that Heinz is desperate in such a situation and wants to do everything possible to save his wife. Nevertheless, it is not acceptable to commit a crime such as burglary and theft in order to obtain the medication.

Instead, Heinz should look for alternative ways to obtain the medication. Here are some suggestions:
1. Negotiation: Heinz could try to persuade the pharmacist and find a negotiated solution. He could argue that, although he cannot pay the full price, he has managed to raise a considerable amount. The pharmacist might be willing to grant a discount or accept payment in installments.
2. Fundraising: Heinz could start a fundraising campaign to raise the required amount. He could ask friends, family, and acquaintances to donate, and also seek support through social media.
3. Seek public support: Heinz could try to draw attention to his case by contacting local media or starting a petition. This could help put pressure on the pharmacist or find alternative solutions.
4. Contact doctors and hospitals: Heinz could try to contact other doctors or hospitals to see if they have access to similar medications or can suggest alternative treatment methods.
5. Take legal action: If the pharmacist is selling the medication at an excessive price, this could be against the law. Heinz could consult a lawyer to discuss his options.

Reasons for these decisions:
1. Negotiation: A negotiated solution is a peaceful and legal way to reach an agreement. It also shows respect for the pharmacist and his work.

2. Fundraising: Fundraising is a legal and ethical way to collect money for a good cause. It also shows that Heinz is willing to work hard to obtain the medication.
3. Seek public support: Public support can help draw attention to the case and put pressure on the pharmacist to find a solution. It can also help to find alternative solutions, such as having the medication produced by another pharmacy.
4. Contact doctors and hospitals: Doctors and hospitals have access to many resources and could suggest alternative treatments or medications.
5. Take legal action: If the pharmacist is violating the law, this could result in him being forced to sell the medication at a reasonable price. It is important to respect the law and exhaust all legal means before resorting to a crime.

(Source: Mistral Medium; accessed on 27.09.2024)

References

Arnold R (2017) Es ist später, als du denkst. Perspektiven für die Restbiografie. hep Verlag, Bern

Arnold R, Siebert H (2003) Konstruktivistische Erwachsenenbildung, 4. Aufl. Schneider Verlag Hohengehren, Baltmannsweiler

Baum D (2024) Generative AI and LLMs. Wiley, Hoboken

Beck U (1986) Risikogesellschaft. Suhrkamp, Frankfurt am Main

Clutterbuck D (2022) The future of AI in coaching. In: Greif S, Möller H, Scholl W, Passmore J, Müller F (Hrsg) International handbook of evidence-based coaching: theory, research and practice. Springer Nature, Cham, S 369–379

Damasio A (2017) Am Anfang war das Gefühl. Siedler, München

DiGirolamo JA (2024) The potential for artificial intelligence in coaching. In: Passmore J, Diller SJ, Isaacson S, Brantl M (Hrsg) The Digital and AI Coaches' Handbook. Routledge, London/New York, S 276–285

Edenhausen (2024) Coaching und Beratung treffen auf KI. In: Der systemische Ansatz in Zeiten von ChatGPT. Selbstverlag, Innsbruck

Geißler H (2017) Die Grammatik des Coachens. Springer, Wiesbaden

Habermas J (1981) Theorie des kommunikativen Handelns, Bd 2. Suhrkamp, Frankfurt am Main

Harari YN (2024) Nexus. eine kurze Geschichte der Informationsnetzwerke von der Steinzeit bis zur künstlichen Intelligenz. Pinguin, München

Kaplan A, Haenlein M (2019) Siri, Siri, in my hand: who's the fairest in the land? On the interpretations, illustrations, and implications of artifical intelligence. Business Horizons 62(1):15–25

Lämpe C (2024) Epochen der Künstlichen Intelligenz: Die Entwicklung Künstlicher Neuronaler Netze. ► https://www.like-us.me/nampus. Zugegriffen am 17.10.2024

Luhmann N (1984) Soziale Systeme. Suhrkamp, Frankfurt am Main

Nielsen MA (2023) Neural networks and deep learning. Springer, Wiesbaden

Oser F, Althof W (1992) Moralische Selbstbestimmung. Klett-Cotta, Stuttgart

Prange K (1978) Pädagogik als Erfahrungsprozess. 1. Der pädagogische Aufbau der Erfahrung. Klett-Cotta, Stuttgart

Searle RJ (1971) Sprechakte. Ein sprachphilosophischer Essay. Suhrkamp, Frankfurt am Main

Watzlawick P, Beavin JH, Jackson DD (1969) Menschliche Kommunikation. Hans Huber, Bern/Stuttgart/Wien

Wilson EO (2013) Die soziale Eroberung der Erde. Eine biologische Geschichte des Menschen. Beck, München

Wittgenstein L (1971a) Tractatus logico-philosophicus. Logisch-philosophische Abhandlung. Suhrkamp, Frankfurt am Main

Wittgenstein L (1971b) Philosophische Untersuchungen. Suhrkamp, Frankfurt am Main

Conceptual Foundations of Coaching

Contents

H. Geissler, *AI-Coaching*,
https://doi.org/10.1007/978-3-658-49178-9_3

3.1 What is Coaching?

Although coaching can now look back on several decades of highly successful practical development, and the scope and plurality of academic work is also impressive (see, e.g., Bachkirova et al. 2017; Greif et al. 2022; Passmore et al. 2013), it has not yet been possible to develop a generally accepted definition of coaching (Greif 2021).

On the other hand, there has so far been broad consensus about what coaching is *not.* There was widespread agreement that coaching is an independent format, due to its distinction on the one hand from psychotherapy and on the other from qualification, i.e., training of practical skills and instruction in domain-specific knowledge.

However, even this residual consensus is threatened by the current intersections of artificial intelligence with coaching. According to Passmore, Diller, Isaacson, and Brantl (2024, p. 9), these developments cause the significance and transmission of domain-specific knowledge to appear in a new light.

The consequence of these new developments is that the previously unsatisfactorily answered question of how to define coaching conceptually can no longer be set aside. This is perhaps one of the most valuable impulses resulting from the incursion of artificial intelligence into the field of coaching (Bachkirova and Kemp 2024, p. 2).

This challenge will be addressed below by first attempting to identify those individual characteristics that are relatively undisputed in the coaching discourse (Bachkirova et al. 2017; Greif et al. 2022). In this sense, it can be stated,

- that coaching is a *help-offering practice* for people (coachees) with *professional and/or personal problems or challenges,*
- which they have so far been unable to solve satisfactorily in their practice, despite more or less intensive and prolonged attempts,
- whereby it must be emphasized or ensured at the beginning of coaching that the causes of these problems, or the reason they have not yet been satisfactorily resolved, are *not psychological disorders.*
- These problems or challenges can be described as *differences between the coachees' perceived actual situation and their desired target situation.*
- On this basis, the primary goal of coaching is to stimulate and support coachees to *develop solutions on their own initiative*
- to *develop and implement needs-based solutions* for their problems or challenges.
- For this purpose, they are offered a *protected space* that stands in contrast to the problems or challenges of their everyday life.
- In coaching processes that take place in these spaces—face-to-face, online, with or without artificial intelligence—decisions must be made that can be assigned to four decision areas. Specifically, it must be decided,
  - which aspects of the current actual situation, the desired target situation, and previous or future goal-oriented activities should become the *content* of reflection and communication,

- which *media* should be used and how, in order to transfer the problems experienced in the coachees' everyday life—that is, problematic content—from everyday life into the coaching practice, and vice versa,
- by means of which *methods* the process of reflection and communicative discussion of coaching content should be guided,
- and towards which *goals* the methodically structured and media-facilitated reflection and communicative discussion of coaching content should be directed.

With regard to these characteristics, there is a relatively broad consensus in the coaching discourse that they are fundamental to coaching. However, it remains unclear and contested what is meant by *needs-based solutions.* Behind this question lies the *coaching alignment problem,* with the requirement to sufficiently consider the values and interests of the coachees.

This problem is addressed differently in coaching theory and practice and has led to the development of two different basic conceptions of coaching.

The first of these two basic conceptions focuses exclusively on the *interpersonal dimension of the coaching alignment problem* and obliges coaches accordingly to respect the values of the coachees and, on this basis, to understand coaching as a service that consists in helping coachees *instrumentally* to achieve their desired goals as effectively as possible.

The alternative conception is that coaching must also be oriented toward meaningful personal development. The coaching alignment problem must therefore be conceptually broadened by sufficiently considering, in addition to the *interpersonal dimension,* the *intrapersonal dimension* as well (see Fig. 3.1). The fundamental task of coaching is therefore to mediate between the situational needs and goals of the coachees and the possibilities for their positive personal development, regardless of whether or to what extent the coachees are aware of the latter.

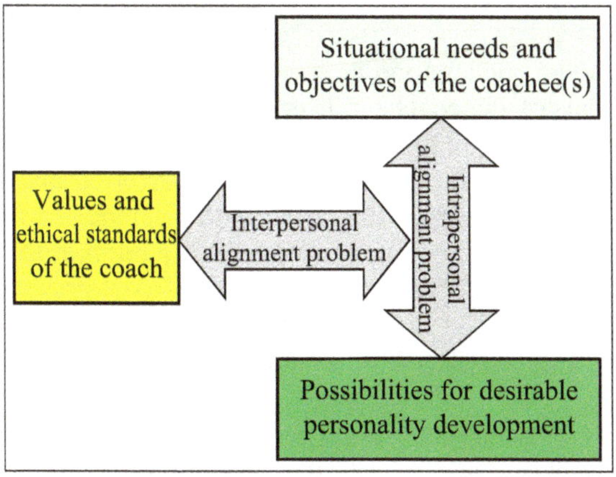

Fig. 3.1 The double alignment problem in coaching

3

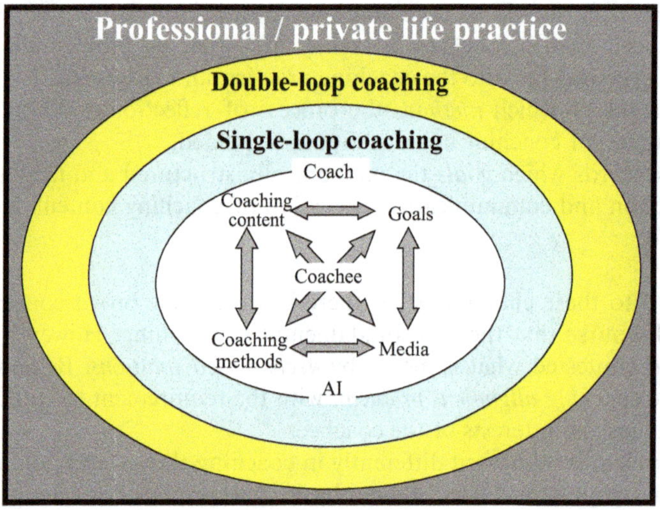

Fig. 3.2 Single-loop Coaching und Double-loop Coaching

With the proposal of such an additional reflection loop, reference is made to the *theory of organizational learning* developed by Argyris und Schön (1978) and its underlying distinction between *single-loop learning* and *double-loop learning*.

As shown in Fig. 3.2, two fundamental concepts can therefore be distinguished in the context of coaching: *Single-loop Coaching,* which is understood as a service and thus focuses solely on the interpersonal dimension of the alignment problem, and *Double-loop Coaching,* which is understood as a process of meaning-making related to personal development and therefore also takes into account the intrapersonal dimension of the alignment problem.

3.1.1 Single-loop Coaching

Single-loop Coaching is understood as a service, which obligates coaches to serve the wishes and goals of the coachees. It is therefore considered a transgression if coaches question the coaching goals of their coachees. Rather, the current needs and target expectations of the coachees must be perceived and used as unproblematic reference points in order to clarify, with reference to them, which facts and interrelations of the present actual situation are relevant to the problem and can be perceived as resources for the development of goal-oriented activities.

Ideally, this results in four areas of responsibility, which are embedded in an overarching context to be reflected upon and designed in a purpose-rational manner, namely:

- to capture the existing target expectations as precisely as possible,
- in order to analyze the existing conditions with regard to these expectations and to determine how favorable or unfavorable the various factors or

constellations of factors are for achieving the goals, or how realistic the coachees' target expectations are.
- These insights then form the basis for the development of goal-oriented strategies, decisions, and activities,
- the subsequent implementation of which must be supported accordingly.

On this basis, the processes relating to the interrelationships of coaching content, goals, methods, and media can be largely *standardized and routinized* on the basis of *purpose-rationality,* so that they can also be carried out by an AI agent.

Such routinization can be conceptually implemented in different ways. For example, it can be based on the GROW model proposed by Whitmore (1992) or the solution-focused coaching model developed by de Shazer (e.g., Szabó and Berg 2006). The concept of client-centered communication advocated by Rogers (Stober 2006) can also be used as a basis, as can the psychology of behaviorism (Eldridge and Dembkowski 2013), the basic understanding of cognitive psychology (Auerbach 2006), or that of cognitive-behavioral psychology (Palmer and Williams 2013).

Based on single-loop coaching, three options arise regarding the question of whether and how artificial intelligence can be used in or for coaching:

The first option is to *reject the use of artificial intelligence* in any form. There are, ideally, four reasons or arguments for this:
- The first and probably most common reason is adherence to what has proven effective so far.
- This reason can be combined with a second, namely a lack of experience or proficiency in dealing with the relevant technology.
- Third, the argument of data-related risks may also be added.
- And a fourth argument could be the conviction that personal, interpersonal contact is a prerequisite for coaching, and that the use of artificial intelligence is therefore perceived as an unacceptable disruption.

The second—and completely opposite—option is to *replace human coaches with AI agents.* There can also be various reasons for this:
- A first reason could be the extremely low cost of such coaching, as well as the unlimited 24/7 availability of corresponding AI agents.
- Another reason could be that coachees find it easier to approach an AI agent, especially when dealing with topics associated with shame.
- A third reason could be that coachees are primarily interested in good substantive input or objective feedback, and not so much in a personal relationship with a coach.
- Finally, this usage option is also available to coaches themselves, to prepare for coaching sessions or to receive supervision regarding sessions that have already taken place.

With regard to this second usage variant, Graßmann and Schermuly (2021, p. 109) define AI coaching as "a machine-assisted, systematic process to help clients set professional goals and construct solutions to efficiently achieve them."

The third usage variant is ultimately a combination of the first two. Coachees can independently prepare for a coaching session with a coach using an AI agent, or coaches can encourage their coachees to conduct an AI coaching session between two meetings in order to systematically test the insights from the coaching session in practice (Mai and Rutschmann 2023a, b).

3.1.2 Double-loop Coaching

The alternative to single-loop coaching is *double-loop coaching.* It has a clear affinity with *educational philosophy* and *pedagogical anthropology,* which assume that the essence of the human being has the *structure of an open question,* i.e., a question that connects knowledge and non-knowledge in a specific way (Prange 1978). Based on this premise, the central task of the human being is to determine themselves with the help of their capacity for normative and value rationality, and to implement the resulting goals in an instrumental-rational manner. Self-determination therefore always consists of two parts, which are circularly connected: the development and review of desired goals guided by normative and value rationality, and their subsequent implementation in practice through instrumental rationality.

Double-loop coaching is therefore a *meaning-clarifying coaching as personality development* (see, e.g.: Berninger-Schäfer 2018; Bachkirova 2022; Diamond 2013; Eidenschink 2006; Freire 2013; Geißler 2017; Greif 2021; Schmidt 2004; Spoth et al. 2013; Stelter 2013).

In this context, the question of how coaches can manage the processes of such coaching is particularly important.

Gunther Schmidt answered this question in a video lecture from the "life lessons" media series, which is unfortunately no longer available, referring to the "*control position*" that must be assumed. This consists of the consciously induced and controlled imagination that one is in a semi-permeable protected space, bounded by a bell-shaped energy field that prevents unpleasant things from penetrating, but at the same time is permeable enough to allow for intensive, differentiated contact with the coachees and to maintain it. Schmidt describes this protected space for observation and experience as a space in which one has *emotional and bodily experiences,*

> "standing firmly, calm within oneself and optimally balanced on the ground, with a strengthened back, being empathetically capable of action, powerful and smoothly flexible, and looking in all directions with an open, curious gaze."

However, the energy field of this imagined space not only serves a protective function, but also acts as a kind of *canvas* onto which the coachees project their problems, so that the coaches can perceive them in a protected and safe, yet also curious and empathetically engaged manner. In this way, they gain access to

> "their vast involuntary knowledge repertoire, which has developed in them over the course of their lives, with everything they have learned cognitively and intuitively.

> The use of this involuntary knowledge repertoire, together with their consciously acquired experiential and conceptual knowledge, provides them with an optimal sense of coherence."

On this basis, it then becomes possible to develop *hypotheses* and project them onto this canvas in order to observe and examine them in the manner described above. In this context—as Schmidt's line of argument can be extended—it is reasonable to use artificial intelligence and have it develop hypotheses, which can then be deliberately projected onto this canvas and examined.

These explanations make two things clear: first, how important it is for double-loop coaching that the relationship coaches have with their coachees is fundamentally shaped by the relationship they have with themselves. Second, it becomes clear that, in shaping this dual relationship, one's own *emotional and bodily perceptions* and those of the coachees are essential and must be connected with one's own rational and intuitive thinking and actions, as well as with those of the coachees.

With regard to the possible use of artificial intelligence for such a theoretically grounded double-loop coaching, in contrast to single-loop coaching, there are two options:

As with single-loop coaching, the first option is to completely refrain from using AI, for the same reasons already mentioned above.

The second option is to systematically integrate AI into the coach-coachee dialogue, for example by following the model presented in Chapter 8. The main reason for this is to increase the value of coaching by involving an AI-supported coach assistant. As will be shown in detail in Chapter 8, the special capabilities of such AI assistants lie in their ability to process the information provided to them about the coaching topic in relation to given criteria extremely quickly and without possible emotional distortion, thus offering valuable suggestions for problem analysis and the development of possible solutions.

3.2 Coaching Methods and Artificial Intelligence

Coaching methods, i.e., the procedures for the processual structuring of reflection and the communicative thematization of coaching content and goals, are fundamental for both single-loop coaching and double-loop coaching.

In order to clarify which coaching methods can be shaped by AI agents, to what extent, and in what manner, it is useful to refer back to the task of coaches, which was only briefly mentioned in the previous section but not further elaborated: to encourage their coachees to engage with their previously less successful *problem-solving activities* in order to discover more successful alternatives that enable them to develop and consistently implement self-determined, tailored problem-solving strategies.

As shown in ◘ Fig. 3.3, the following *psychological problem-processing activities* are particularly important in this context (Geißler and Rödel 2023, pp. 78 ff.):

3

- *Rational thinking:* Coachees use—more or less successfully—their cognitive abilities to identify and analyze the individual characteristics and interrelationships that are important for the current actual situation, the intended target situation, and the measures and activities for achieving the goal.
- *Intuitive thinking:* Coachees use—more or less successfully—their ability to recall, in a vivid and differentiated way, problematic and successful situations and events, as well as their ability to vividly and in a differentiated manner imagine successful management of situations and processes.
- *Rational action control:* Coachees use—more or less successfully—their abilities to align their actions with specific goals and values and with the problem-solving ideas or concepts they have developed, and to control them rationally with reference to these.
- *Intuitive action control:* Coachees use—more or less successfully—their abilities to intuitively grasp the problem-solving relevant courses of action in certain situations and processes and to implement them in practice.
- *Experiences of being befallen and self-efficacy:* Coachees engage—more or less successfully—on the one hand with what has happened to them and has made them the object of adverse circumstances and processes, and on the other hand with the events that they were largely able to determine themselves.
- *Emotional and bodily experiences:* Coachees use—more or less successfully—the emotions and bodily experiences they have had in dealing with actual and imagined situations and processes of success and failure.

As already mentioned, coachees apply these six psychological problem-processing activities suboptimally in their everyday lives as experienced as problematic. The task facing both human coaches and AI agents that support or replace them

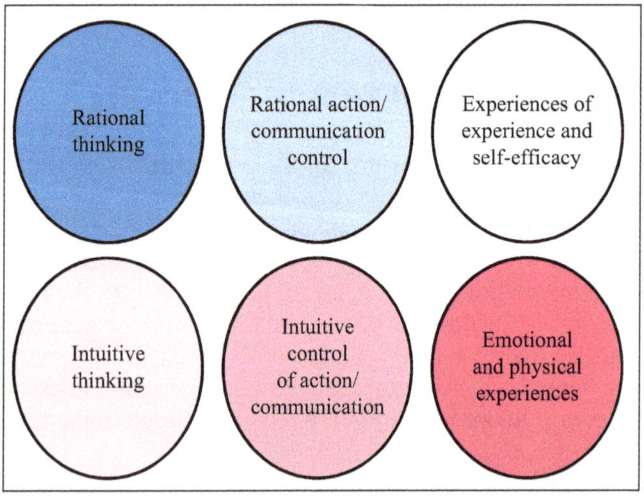

Fig. 3.3 The psychological problem-processing activities that are fundamental both for the coachees' everyday practice and for the coaching process. (Geißler and Rödel 2023, p. 89)

is therefore to use appropriate coaching methods—such as coaching questions, feedback, role plays, etc.—to prompt coachees to apply more suitable psychological problem-processing activities in the right way.

For this purpose, human coaches use their ability to empathically think and feel themselves into their coachees and, on this basis, to explore which psychological problem-processing activities are meaningful to use and in what way. They can then use this imagined self-experience as a basis for certain coaching-methodical behaviors, such as formulating specific coaching questions, providing concise summaries of what has been perceived, and so on.

These interrelations make the limitations of AI clear. Chatbots and AI agents do not have the ability to have embodied experiences of being befallen and self-efficacy, nor the associated emotional and bodily experiences, and therefore cannot act empathically on this basis.

However, they can compensate for this limitation in their coaching-methodical design options by acting as if they were acting empathically.

On this basis, two questions arise: first, how well coachees can (or cannot) perceive this, and second, how much it bothers them if they do perceive it.

3.3 Coaching Media and Artificial Intelligence

Coaching methods are closely linked to *coaching media* (Geißler and Rödel 2023). While the former shape the process of how the content of a given coaching issue is to be meaningfully reflected upon and communicated, the coaching media are, so to speak, the *containers for the coaching content* that must be transferred from everyday practice into coaching practice in order to be methodically processed there. In this context, the question arises as to whether chatbots or AI agents can take on the function of coaching media and how they relate to other coaching media.

To answer this question, it is useful to first take a look at the coaching media available to date and to distinguish between two basic types of coaching media: *physical and psychological coaching media* (Geißler and Rödel 2023).

The latter refer to the psychological conditions and possibilities of the psychological problem-processing activities presented in the previous section. The former, as the name suggests, are characterized by certain physical features.

Specifically, two groups can be distinguished here: *coaching communication media* and *coaching problem-solving media* (Geißler 2018). In relation to this distinction, the question arises as to whether chatbots or AI agents are technological innovations that belong to the category of coaching communication media, or whether they represent new coaching problem-solving media.

3.3.1 Coaching Communication Media

To answer this question, let us first look at the available coaching communication media (see ◘ Fig. 3.4). These can be divided into natural and digital media.

3

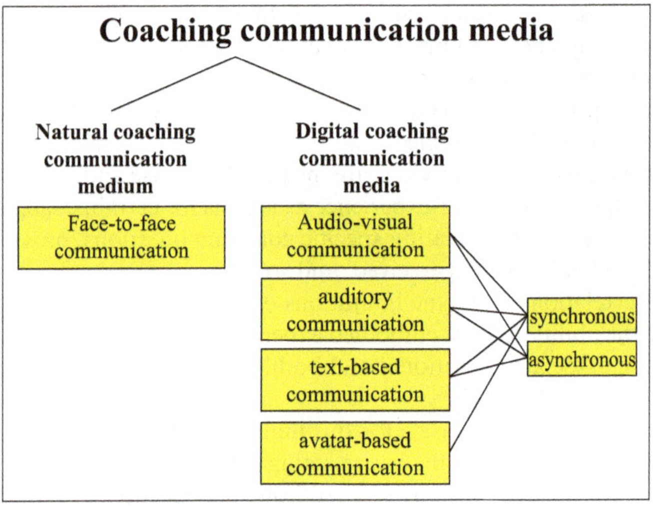

Fig. 3.4 The various coaching communication media

The natural coaching communication media include

- face-to-face communication
- and (although only extremely rarely used) letter-based communication.

The area of digital coaching communication media, which may also include chatbots and AI agents, is currently divided into

- synchronous audio-visual,
- asynchronous audio-visual,
- synchronous auditory,
- asynchronous auditory,
- synchronous text-based
- and asynchronous text-based communication media (Geißler 2018; Geißler and Rödel 2023).

As a special case, synchronous avatar-based communication may also be added here, in which coach and coachee use digital platforms such as Second Life and present themselves to each other in the form of avatars (Andrews 2014). However, since its use is still technically very complex, this communication medium is hardly used at all so far.

With regard to this structural outline, one might get the impression that AI-based textual and verbal communication, from a media theory perspective, represents a new development in the areas of synchronous text and audio communication.

However, this thought immediately provokes the critical observation that communication media have so far been defined by the characteristic that they enable a communicative connection, i.e., the exchange of cognitive content—information, opinions, and intentions—as well as the establishment and shaping of an emotional relationship (bonding) between different people. But this does not apply to AI-based communication. Here, people are communicating with machines.

For this reason, it makes sense to examine whether, from a media theory perspective, AI-based communication should be assigned to the group of physical coaching problem-solving media.

3.3.2 Coaching Problem-Solving Media

To answer this question, it is again useful to first take a look at the field of existing physical coaching problem-solving media. These are divided into the following segments (Berninger-Schäfer 2018; Geißler 2018; Geißler and Rödel 2023):

- *Text-based problem-solving media:* The following variants are available here (Mundelsee and Sawatzki 2022):
  - completely unlabelled media (such as index cards or flipcharts or digital whiteboards) that can be written on;
  - physical or digital materials that are partially labelled, e.g., with questions, statements, or cloze texts, and prompt the user to answer the questions in writing, formulate responses to the statements, or complete the cloze texts;
  - or physical or digital texts that do not allow for one's own written input.

  These physical problem-solving media are well suited to stimulate
  - *rational reflection processes,* namely by
    - conducting problem analyses in writing
    - and/or using existing texts for problem analysis or for identifying problem-solving activities,
  - and/or to stimulate *intuitive reflection processes,* namely by
    - writing down important experiences in a way that is rich in lived experience
    - and/or reading written narratives or fantasy stories.
- *Image-based problem-solving media:* That is, the coachees view and experience images, either physical or digital, under the guidance of their coach (Messerschmidt 2015).

  These physical problem-solving media are well suited to stimulate
  - *intuitive reflection processes,* namely by mentally immersing themselves in the image
  - and thereby experiencing certain *emotions or bodily sensations.*
- *Material objects or virtual worlds with avatars:* That is, the coachees work with physical objects (e.g., stones or wooden figures as part of a constellation exercise), which they position in space or (in the case of modeling clay) shape physically, or they position avatars at certain locations in a virtual world and design them in terms of their external appearance and, if applicable, their body movements and facial expressions (Tawadros et al. 2018).

  These physical problem-solving media are well suited
  - to stimulate processes of *rational and intuitive action control* by having the coachees orient themselves rationally or intuitively to a specific design task
  - and in the process have certain *experiences of being befallen and self-efficacy* as well as *emotional and bodily experiences.*

With regard to this structure, it seems reasonable to assign text-based and verbal AI-based communication to the segment of text-based coaching problem-solving media and to enrich it accordingly. – This proposed assignment is also justified in view of the history of coaching media, which will be presented below.

3.4 Historical Conceptualization of AI Coaching in Coaching Practice

A look at the—short—history of coaching makes it clear that the question of whether chatbots or AI agents can replace human coaches was already being discussed, in a slightly different form, two decades ago (Geißler 2024). Under the title "Does Coaching Need a Coach?" Martina Offermanns published her dissertation in 2004, in which she empirically examined the effectiveness of *self-coaching.* She refers to self-coaching in which "the consultant provides the coachee with coaching materials tailored to their individual topic and only supports them in the scheduling of the agreed sessions" (Offermanns 2004, p. 130), while "the content design of the sessions (…) is exclusively the responsibility of the coachees" (ibid.).

In a very similar way, Harald Geißler shortly thereafter developed a "Virtual Coaching (VC)" approach, in the form of a set of fundamental coaching questions organized into several thematic blocks, which coachees are required to answer in writing in a specific sequence (Geißler et al. 2007). The following example (◘ Table 3.1) relates to clarifying the current coaching needs and demonstrates how coachees can be stimulated and guided by such sets of questions to reflect methodically and systematically on their coaching topics, relating various aspects to each other in such a way that their perspective opens up to previously unrecognized solution possibilities.

Looking back at the developments and discussions of that time, one quickly recognizes parallels to our current debate about the relationship between AI and coaching. Even then, there was considerable excitement, as there were concerns that digital self-coaching tools would harm the still nascent coaching practice.

The first important similarity that stands out when comparing "Virtual Coaching (VC)" with coaching-specific AI agents such as "Vici" or "Alpina" is that coachees engage with textual artifacts that—virtually—have people behind them who developed them, without these individuals personally appearing in the coaching process.

The crucial difference, however, is that coaching-specific AI agents are also capable of concisely summarizing the responses they receive, placing them in broader thematic contexts, asking follow-up questions that further develop the content, and making solution-oriented suggestions. And, even more importantly: in their interactions with coachees, they can improve their conversational skills, i.e., they can use their experiences to *learn.*

Let us now look at the *developmental bridge* that connects the self-coaching tools developed two decades ago with the coaching bots currently available. Even

Table 3.1 Question set for clarifying current coaching needs

What do I ultimately want? (Outcome goal) What is the outcome goal of my coaching, i.e., what should change positively in my life as a result of the coaching, and by when? – ??? How large—expressed on a scale from 0 to 10—is the gap between the desired and current state, i.e., the difference between the outcome goal and the current situation? – ??? What percentage of my coaching outcome goal relates a) to my professional life, b) to my private life, and c) to my health? – ??? If I achieve my outcome goal 100%, how strongly—expressed on a scale from 0 to 10—will this positively impact each of the three areas mentioned above? – ???	**Importance, difficulty, and pressure** How important—expressed on a scale from 0 to 10—is the positive change mentioned in the left column to me? (10 = extremely important) – ??? How difficult—expressed on a scale from 0 to 10—is it to achieve the positive change mentioned in the left column? (9 = extremely difficult but achievable. 10 = not achievable) – ??? How much pressure—expressed on a scale from 0 to 10—do I feel because the positive change mentioned in the left column has not yet occurred? (10 = extremely high) – ??? What percentage of this pressure is generated by others and what percentage by myself? – ??? To what extent—expressed as a percentage—does the complete achievement of the desired positive change depend on me? – ???
Solution ideas How clearly—expressed on a scale from 0 to 10—do I know what I no longer want to endure/do? (10 = absolutely clear) – ??? How clearly—expressed on a scale from 0 to 10—do I know what should change positively in the near future? (10 = absolutely clear) – ???	**Solution activities** How clearly—expressed on a scale from 0 to 10—do I know exactly what I need to do to achieve my outcome goal? (10 = absolutely clear) – ??? How important—expressed on a scale from 0 to 10—is it for me to also develop personally in the process? (10 = absolutely clear) – ???
Desire for support How important/unimportant—expressed on a scale from 0 to 10—is it for me to have a coach who helps me clarify my ideas or critically review my thoughts? (10 = extremely important) – ??? How important/unimportant—expressed on a scale from 0 to 10—is it for me to have a coach who repeatedly encourages me to consistently implement what I have set out to do? (10 = extremely important) – ???	**Indicators of success** How can I clearly recognize that my (self-) coaching has been successful? – ???

before the development of generative artificial intelligence with its ability to process natural language and learn autonomously, coaching bots were built—based on *digital decision trees.* These were based on standardized process steps defined by predetermined, often branching statements, such as questions. This means that which question is asked at which point in the coaching process depends on how the user answered the previous question. Each question is therefore invisibly linked to predefined answer options for the user, which—like a switch—determine which question will be asked next.

In view of these historical developments, the assessment is confirmed that chatbots and AI agents can and must be regarded as a *new generation of digital coaching media.*

Finally, there is another reason to recall the media theory discussions that took place two decades ago in connection with the emergence of digital coaching. From a media theory perspective, one can distinguish between *coaching-specific* media, such as "Virtual Coaching," and coaching-*non*-specific media, i.e., media that were not developed specifically for coaching and are sometimes used for entirely different purposes, such as whiteboards.

This differentiation is particularly relevant to our current discussion, as it is not only coaching-specific AI agents that are used for or in coaching, but also coaching-*non*-specific chatbots, such as ChatGPT, Bing, or Gemini.

Given this historical background, it is reasonable to define *AI coaching* as follows:

Definition of AI Coaching

AI coaching refers to self-coaching and/or video call-based coach-coachee dialogues in which artificial intelligence is used as a *coaching problem-solving medium,* either in the form of a coaching-*non*-specific chatbot, such as ChatGPT, whose use must be guided by coaching-specific instructions (prompts), or in the form of a coaching-specific AI agent.

In contrast to traditional digital coaching problem-solving media, chatbots or AI agents used in or for coaching are characterized by their ability to interact with users and to learn in the process.

References

Andrews AR (2014) Avatar coaching: a case study on the perception of virtual coaching interventions with an avatar coach. Unpublished Doctoral Dissertation, Capella University, USA

Argyris C, Schön D (1978) Organizational learning: a theory of action perspective. Addison-Wesley, Reading/Mass.

Auerbach JE (2006) Cognitve Coaching. In: Stober DR, Grant AM (Hrsg) Evidence based coaching handbook: putting best practices to work for your client. Wiley, New York, S 103–128

Bachkirova T (2022) Developmental coaching: working with the self, 2. Aufl. McGrow Hill, New York

Bachkirova T, Kemp R (2024) 'AI coaching': democratizing coaching service or offering an ersatz? Coaching Inter J Theory Res Pract. ▶ https://doi.org/10.1080/17521882.2024.2368598

Bachkirova T, Spence G, Drake D (Hrsg) (2017) The SAGE handbook of coaching. Sage, Los Angelos

Berninger-Schäfer E (2018) Online-coaching. Springer, Wiesbaden

Diamond MA (2013) Psychodynamik approach. In: Passmore J, Peterson DB, Freire T (Hrsg) The Wiley-Blackwell handbook of the psychology of coaching and mentoring. Wiley-Blackwell, Chichester, S 365–384

Eidenschink K (2006) Der einäugige Riese: ‚Lösungsorientiertes Coaching'. Vom Unsinn einer problematischen Fokussierung. Z Organisationsentwickl, Superv, Coach 13(2):153–164

Eldridge F, Dembkowski S (2013) Behavioral coaching. In: Passmore J, Peterson DB, Freire T (Hrsg) The Wiley-Blackwell handbook of the psychology of coaching and mentoring. Wiley-Blackwell, Chichester, S 298–318

Freire T (2013) Positive psychology approaches. In: Passmore J, Peterson DB, Freire T (Hrsg) The Wiley-Blackwell handbook of the psychology of coaching and mentoring. Wiley-Blackwell, Chichester, S 426–442

Geißler H (2017) Die Grammatik des Coachens. Springer, Wiesbaden

Geißler H (2018) E-Coaching – ein Überblick. In: Greif S, Möller H, Scholl W (Hrsg) Handbuch Schlüsselkonzepte im Coaching. Springer, Wiesbaden, S 115–124

Geißler H (2024) KI-Coaching. Die neue Generation der Coaching-Medien. Trainingaktuell Mai 2024, S 11–14, Bonn: ManagerSeminare

Geißler H, Rödel S (2023) Praxishandbuch professionelles Online-Coaching. Beltz, Weinheim/Basel

Geißler H, Helm M, Nolze A (2007) Virtuelles Selbstcoaching – Konzept und erste Erfahrungen. Z Organisationsentwickl, Superv, Coach 13(1):81–93

Graßmann C, Schermuly CC (2021) Coaching with Artificial Intelligence: concepts and capabilities. Human Res Develop Rev 20(1):106–126. ► https://doi.org/10.1177/1534484320982891

Greif S (2021) Was ist Coaching? Wissenschaftliche Grundlagen und praktische Methoden. S. Greif, Osnabrück

Greif S, Möller H, Passmore SW, J. & Müller, F. (Hrsg) (2022) International handbook of evidence-based coaching. Theory, Research and Practice. Springer Nature, Cham

Mai V, Rutschmann R (2023a) Chatbots im Coaching. Potenziale und Einsatzmöglichkeiten von digitalen Coaching-Begleitern und Assistenten. Z Organisationsentwickl, Superv, Coach 30:45–57. ► https://link.springer.com/article/10.1007/s11613-022-00801-3. Zugriffsdatum an. 10.07.2024

Mai V, Rutschmann R (2023b) Best Practices im Chatbot Coaching. Einblicke in Forschung und Entwicklung des StudiCoachBots der TH Köln und in die Coaching Chatbot Plattform evoach. Z Organisationsentwickl, Superv, Coach 30:111–125. ► https://doi.org/10.1007/s11613-022-00802-2

Messerschmidt J (2015) Das Selbst im Bild. Peter Lang, Frankfurt am Main

Mundelsee L, Sawatzki D (2022) 50 Coaching-Karten Blended Coaching & Counceling. Beltz, Weinheim/Basel

Offermanns M (2004) Braucht Coaching einen Coach? Eine evaluative Pilotstudie. ibidem, Stuttgart

Palmer S, Williams HS (2013) Cognitive behavioral coaching. In: Passmore J, Peterson DB, Freire T (Hrsg) The Wiley-Blackwell handbook of the psychology of coaching and mentoring. Wiley-Blackwell, Chichester, S 319–338

Passmore J, Peterson DB, Freire T (Hrsg) (2013) The Wiley-Blackwell handbook of the psychology of coaching and mentoring. Wiley-Blackwell, Chichester

Passmore J, Diller SJ, Isaacson S, Brantl M (2024) Coaching in the digital era. In: Passmore J, Diller SJ, Isaacson S, Brantl M (Hrsg) The Digital and AI Coaches' Handbook. Routledge, London/New York, S 1–17

Prange K (1978) Pädagogik als Erfahrungsprozess. Klett/Cotta, Stattgart

Schmidt G (2004) Liebesaffären zwischen Problem und Lösung. Carl Auer, Heidelberg

Spoth J, Toman S, Leichtman R, Allan J (2013) Gestalt approach. In: Passmore J, Peterson DB, Freire T (Hrsg) The Wiley-Blackwell handbook of the psychology of coaching and mentoring. Wiley-Blackwell, Chichester, S 385–406

Stelter R (2013) Narrative approaches. In: Passmore J, Peterson DB, Freire T (Hrsg) The Wiley-Blackwell handbook of the psychology of coaching and mentoring. Wiley-Blackwell, Chichester, S 407–425

Stober DR (2006) Coaching from the humanistic perspective. In: Stober DR, Grant AM (Hrsg) Evidence based coaching handbook: putting best practices to work for your client. Wiley, New York, S 17–50

Szabó P, Berg IK (2006) Kurz(zeit)coaching mit Langzeitwirkung. SolArgent Media, Basel

Tawadros T, Tinker D, Jackson A (2018) Coaching in a virtual world – Your avatar will see you now. In: Heller J, Triebel C, Hauser B, Koch A (Hrsg) Digitale Medien im Coaching. Springer, Wiesbaden, S 129–137

Whitmore J (1992) Coaching for performance: a practical guide to growing your won skills. Nicholas Brealey Publishing, London

General Design and Application Possibilities of AI In and For Coaching

Contents

H. Geissler, *AI-Coaching*,
https://doi.org/10.1007/978-3-658-49178-9_4

The aim of this publication is, with regard to the problem of the *Sorcerer's Apprentice* addressed in ▶ Sect. 1.1, to provide a broad overview of the various ways in which artificial intelligence can be used in and for coaching. On this basis, Chapter 8 will introduce and discuss an approach that appears particularly promising: the approach of triadic AI coaching with coaching-diagnostic knowledge and an AI-external prompt script.

For this purpose, this chapter aims to identify the central *design and usage parameters* (◘ Fig. 4.1) underlying the various approaches to AI coaching that will be presented and discussed in the following chapters, and which, in a further developed form, form the basis for the above-mentioned triadic AI coaching.

4.1 Design Parameters

The various ways in which AI can be used in and for coaching can be described using the following design parameters:

- Artificial Intelligence can be used
  - in the form of *classificatory or discriminative AI*
  - or in the form of *generative AI.*
- If the latter is the case, large language models can be used,
  - which contain *general* or
  - *coaching-specific knowledge.*

DESIGN PARAMETERS			USAGE PARAMETERS: dyadic Coach	dyadic Coachee	semi triadic	triadic
Artificial Intelligence		discriminative				
		generative				
Knowledge Base		general				
		specific				
Conversational guidance through ...		AI-internal prompt script				
	AI-external prompts	intuitive AI-prompting				
		AI prompt repository				
		AI prompt script				
		AI/coach prompt script				
Communication modality of the AI		written				
		verbal				
Connection with other digital coaching tools		Texts / graphics				
		Pictures / photos				
		3D-visual tools				

◘ **Abb. 4.1** Design and usage parameters for AI coaching

- Another important design parameter is *conversation management.* Here, too, there are several options:
  - The first is that AI agents are programmed using *AI-internal prompt scripts* so that they take over *conversation management* in interaction with the coachees. Responsibility for this then lies with the developers of the respective AI agents.
  - The alternative is that the chatbots or AI agents used do not have such conversation management competence. Their use is therefore only possible with the help of processing instructions, i.e., *AI-external prompts.* In this case, conversation management—and thus responsibility for the coaching process—lies entirely in the hands of the coaches and/or coachees. Specifically, there are four options here:
    - The first is that users, i.e., coaches and/or coachees, intuitively formulate specific AI prompts according to the situation.
    - They can be supported by a so-called AI prompt repository, i.e., a collection of pre-formulated AI prompts. From this collection, they can select suitable AI prompts and, if necessary, adapt them as needed.
    - The alternative to this is either AI prompt scripts, i.e., pre-formulated AI prompts arranged in a specific sequence that provide an overall framework for the coaching process,
    - or coach/AI prompt scripts, i.e., sequenced instructions addressed on the one hand to the coaches and on the other hand to the chatbot or AI agent.
- The usage potential of the respective chatbot or AI agent is ultimately also determined by
  - whether communication with the chatbot or AI agent can take place
    - in writing
    - and/or orally,
  - and whether it is possible to use certain additional digital coaching tools, such as
    - texts in combination with graphics,
    - digital images
    - and 3D tools, which, for example, offer avatars in virtual worlds that can be used, for instance, for constellation work.

4.2 Usage Parameters

The design of the chatbot or AI agent can be tailored to different *usage formats.* The following three options are available for this purpose:

- The *dyadic* usage format is characterized by the fact that chatbots or AI agents are used by both coachees and coaches as a kind of specialized self-coaching tool.
  - *Coachees* can use this approach to address or resolve their current issues or challenges,

  - and *coaches* can use chatbots or AI agents to prepare for coaching sessions or for supervisory follow-up.
- In addition, chatbots and AI agents can also be used in a *dyadically extended* or *semi-triadic* format. This format is characterized by the fact that coachees use chatbots or AI agents, with or without consultation with their coach, in the period between two coaching sessions (Mai and Rutschmann 2023a, b; Terblanche 2024). In this way, at least to some extent, what was discussed in ▶ Sect. 2.2.1 under the keyword "human-in-the-loop" solution approaches can be realized. This is because coachees can be guided in their use of AI by the questions or tasks set by their coach and then discuss the corresponding experiences and insights with their coach. However, it is essential that the chatbot or AI agent is not used directly within the coaching dialogue itself. This usage format can be described as *semi-triadic,* because, in view of the overall coaching process, three parties are involved—coachee, coach, and chatbot or AI agent—but the direct use of the chatbot or AI agent is limited to the coachees.
- Finally, the *strictly triadic* usage format is characterized by the fact that chatbots or AI agents are designed to be used jointly by coaches and coachees within their coaching dialogue. In this way, they can fully leverage the potential of the "human-in-the-loop" solution approach and thus optimize the quality of their coaching (Clutterbuck 2022, p. 375 ff.; Geißler 2024).

References

Clutterbuck D (2022) The future of AI in coaching. In: Greif S, Möller H, Scholl W, Passmore J, Müller F (Hrsg) International handbook of evidence-based coaching: Theory, research and practice. Springer Nature, Cham, S 369–379

Geißler H (2024) KI-Coaching. Die neue Generation der Coaching-Medien. Trainingaktuell Mai 2024, S 11–14, Bonn: ManagerSeminare

Mai V, Rutschmann R (2023a) Chatbots im Coaching. Potenziale und Einsatzmöglichkeiten von digitalen Coaching-Begleitern und Assistenten. Z Organisationsentwickl, Superv, Coach 30:45–57. ▶ https://link.springer.com/article/10.1007/s11613-022-00801-3. Zugriffsdatum an. 10.07.2024

Mai V, Rutschmann R (2023b) Best Practices im Chatbot Coaching. Einblicke in Forschung und Entwicklung des StudiCoachBots der TH Köln und in die Coaching Chatbot Plattform evoach. Z Organisationsentwickl, Superv, Coach 30:111–125. ▶ https://doi.org/10.1007/s11613-022-00802-2

Terblanche N (2024) Artificial Intelligence (AI) coaching: redefining people development and organizational performance. J Appl Behav Sci:1–8. ▶ https://doi.org/10.1177/00218863241283919. Zugriffsdatum an. 17.07.2024

Non-Coaching-Specific Chatbots and Their Coaching-Specific Use Through External AI Prompts

Contents

H. Geissler, *AI-Coaching*,
https://doi.org/10.1007/978-3-658-49178-9_5

Chatbots such as ChatGPT, Perplexity, Claude, etc., possess a very broad encyclopedic knowledge, which also includes knowledge about coaching. However, this is not their main focus and is not as differentiated as in AI agents designed to replace human coaches. For this reason, they are referred to here—somewhat broadly—as non-coaching-specific chatbots.

With these characteristics, they can be used in two ways: either like coaching AI agents, where the chatbot leads the conversation to provide assistance, or as advisory tools. However, this requires that users provide them with tasks (prompts) and thus take over the conversational lead themselves.

While the first of these two options is discussed in ▶ Sect. 7.1, the following explanations refer exclusively to the second option.

Referring to the structural outline of the previous chapter, the *technical design parameters* of this usage option are characterized as follows (◻ Fig. 5.1):

- that the technical foundation of these chatbots is *generative AI,*
- that their large language models have a *general, i.e., non-coaching-specific knowledge base,*
- and that it is possible to communicate with the chatbots *in writing or orally.*
- A prerequisite for this is that their users, i.e., coachees and coaches, provide the chatbot with coaching-specific tasks. Since these are provided externally to the AI, they can be referred to as *AI-external AI prompts.* Specifically, three options can be distinguished:
  - that coachees or coaches develop these intuitively,
  - that they use a prompt repository, i.e., a collection of pre-formulated prompts, and, if necessary, modify them to fit the situation,
  - or that they follow a prompt script, i.e., a predefined sequence of pre-formulated prompts, with the option to reformulate them to fit the situation as well.

On this basis, the following usage options are available:

- Individuals seeking advice can use them *dyadically* in the role of *coachees* and thus replace human coaches.
- However, *coaches* can also use them *dyadically* by using them to prepare for or follow up on coaching sessions. There are two options for this:
  - The first is that coaches put themselves in the position of their coachees and, in interaction with the chatbot, act as if they were these coachees,
  - or they inform the chatbot of the problem they have as a coach with a particular coachee and ask for help.
- A third option is *semi-triadic usage,* which is characterized by coachees—either with or without consultation with their coach—using non-coaching-specific chatbots to prepare for upcoming coaching sessions, and then discussing the experiences or insights gained with their coaches, without directly integrating the non-coaching-specific chatbot into the coach-coachee dialogue.
- Finally, the fourth option is the *triadic usage in the narrower sense.*

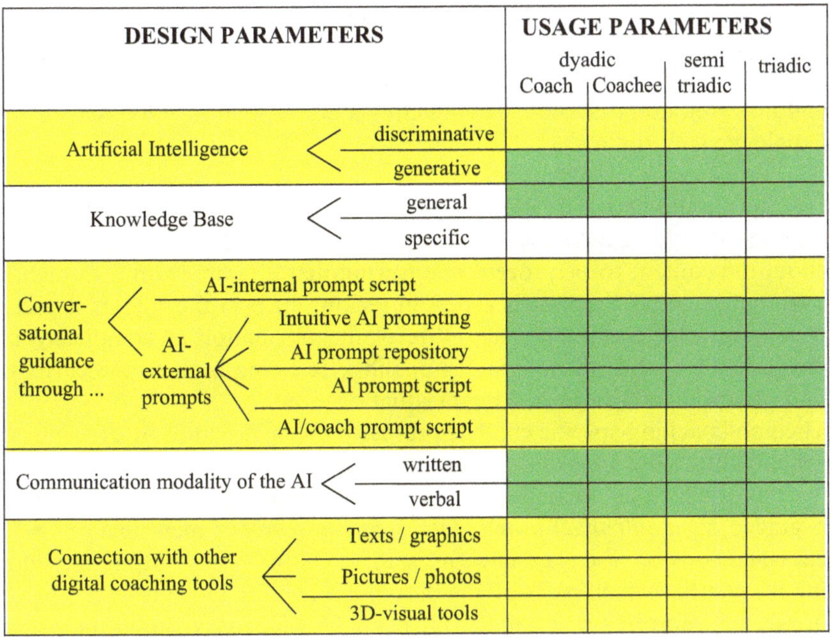

Fig. 5.1 Non-coaching-specific chatbots and their coaching-specific usage options

5.1 Fundamentals

If you want to use non-coaching-specific chatbots for coaching services and wish to manage the conversation yourself, you need to give the respective chatbots meaningful instructions. Since these are essentially provided externally, they can be referred to as *AI-external prompts,* distinguishing them from the AI-internal prompt scripts that are fundamental to most coaching AI agents.

When designing AI-external prompts, it must be taken into account that there are always two components to be designed, namely

- the description of the *content* that the AI is supposed to process,
- and the description of the *output-oriented activity* by which this content should be processed in order to generate a specific output. Formally, the following output-oriented activities are suitable here, namely
  - to check the completeness of the information conveyed in the description of a specific processing content, i.e., to indicate which potentially important information is still missing
  - to summarize the available information using a specific criterion
  - or to analyze it,
  - or to develop a concept based on the information provided,
  - or to offer suggestions for problem-solving.

On this basis, the quality of AI prompts is determined by

- how well, on the one hand, the content to be processed and, on the other hand, the output-oriented processing activities are formulated,
- and how well users succeed in conducting a correspondingly focused chat, i.e., a dialogue with the AI.

5

Such a chat should have the following basic or process structure (Fig. 5.2):

- The first step for the AI user must be to inform the AI, in writing or verbally, about the content to be processed, ensuring that all important information is communicated. If the user is a person seeking help in the role of a coachee, it is important to communicate all relevant information as completely, in as much detail, and as thoroughly as possible, referring both to the current actual situation and the desired target situation.
- The non-coaching-specific chatbot processes this instruction by drawing on its general knowledge base and produces a corresponding output.
- On this basis, the second step for the AI user follows, e.g., the coachee. This is guided by the *"human-in-the-loop" solution approach* mentioned in Sect. 2.2.1 and consists of engaging with the information in this output and informing the chatbot which parts of the output are helpful and can be productively integrated into one's own knowledge base. This feedback should be provided using an AI prompt, which again consists of two parts: first, the feedback is communicated to the chatbot in terms of content, and then this content is linked to the next processing instruction.

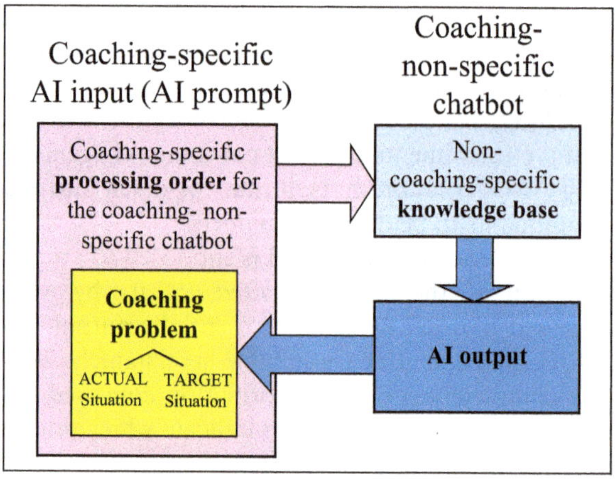

Fig. 5.2 Basic structure of an increasingly specific chat that users (coachees) conduct with non-coaching-specific chatbots using AI prompts

As mentioned above, there are several options for formulating AI prompts:

- The first is to intuitively formulate AI prompts in a situation-specific manner. (See the examples in Edenhausen 2024, pp. 50 ff.).
- As an additional aid, *AI prompt repositories* can be provided, i.e., collections of pre-formulated AI prompts. Users can adopt these as is or adapt them to the specific situation,
- as well as *AI prompt scripts,* i.e., elaborated sequences of pre-formulated AI prompts, which can also be adopted as is or adapted to the specific situation.

With regard to the last two options, it should be noted that they can also be combined. The AI prompts of an AI prompt script can also be used as a collection of AI prompts, with users then determining the order in which they are used.

As will be shown below, there are two types of AI prompts to consider: single-loop and double-loop AI prompts (Fig. 5.3).

With this distinction, we are building on the concept of single-loop and double-loop learning developed by Argyris and Schön (1978).

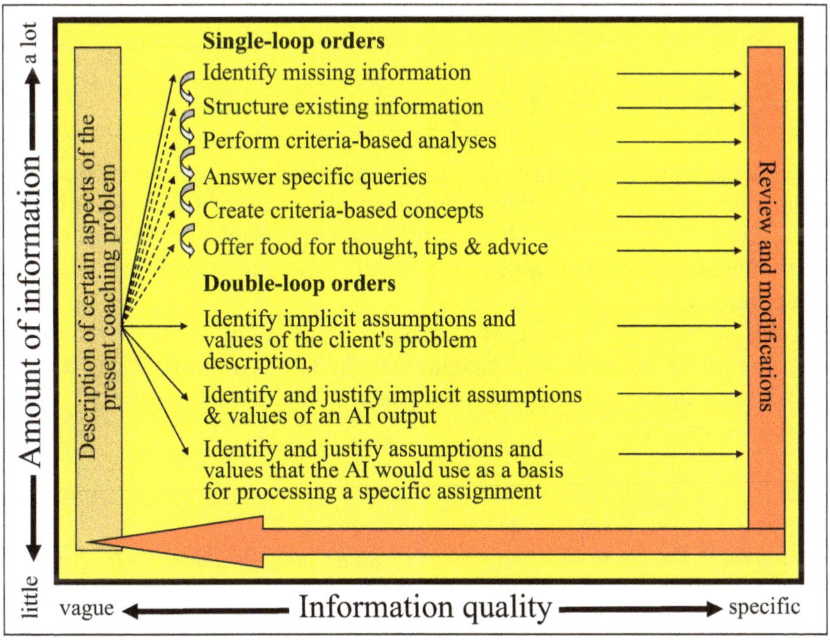

Fig. 5.3 Prompt repository or prompt script with AI-external single-loop prompts and double-loop prompts

5.2 Single-loop AI Prompts

Single-loop AI prompts include content descriptions and processing instructions that—unlike double-loop AI prompts—are not problematized. In terms of a prompt script, the following sequence of six AI prompts is recommended for use in coaching:

- to have the completeness of the information used to describe the present coaching issue checked and to ask whether and which important information might still be missing,
- to have all available information structured in a meaningful way and to have a corresponding report generated,
- on this basis, to ask about the underlying causes of the present issue,
- to ask follow-up questions regarding the information provided by the AI,
- on this basis, to have criteria-based solution concepts developed,
- and finally, to have these specified with suitable impulses, tips, and advice.

These six AI prompts build on each other and therefore form an AI prompt script. However, this does not preclude using them as AI prompts within a prompt repository, i.e., as a collection of useful prompts whose sequence of use is not fixed but can be freely determined by the user.

5.2.1 Identification of Missing Information

When coaches or coachees have sufficiently reflected on the present issue in a differentiated manner, it is advisable to document the result of this reflection in writing, starting with the words: "I have the following problem." To ensure the AI correctly understands this problem, it is helpful to place the subsequent description in parentheses.

On this basis, as part of an AI-external prompt script, it makes sense to first instruct the AI to check the completeness of the information provided and to indicate whether and which important information might still be missing.

Here is an example:

User

I have the following problem:

(I have been working as an IT specialist in a group with ten colleagues for three years. I enjoy the work and get along well with the others. My problem is that a month ago we got a new boss who only puts pressure on us and takes good performance for granted. Although I continue to deliver good results, I receive no recognition for them. On the contrary, he repeatedly makes it clear that the current performance is not sufficient and must be improved. I am not the only one with this problem; the others feel the same way. Since I assume that I cannot change my boss, my only option is to look for another job, either within the company or elsewhere.)

Please check whether any important information might be missing from the above problem description, and tell me what that could be.

AI

The problem description is already quite detailed and provides a good overview of the current situation. Nevertheless, some additional information could be helpful to better understand the situation and identify possible solutions. Here are some aspects that might still be missing:

1. **Specific examples of the boss's criticism:** It would be helpful to know which specific points of criticism the boss has regarding your work and that of the others. Are these points understandable, or do they seem unjustified?
2. **Feedback culture of previous supervisors:** How was recognition and criticism handled before the change in management? Has the feedback culture changed significantly, and if so, how exactly?
3. **Impact on team dynamics:** How is the team responding to the new leadership style? Is there increased tension, declining motivation, or even conflict within the team?
4. **Previous measures and discussions:** Have you or other colleagues already tried to address the issue directly with the boss? If so, how did the conversation go and what was discussed?
5. **Long-term goals and career planning:** What are your long-term goals in your current job? Could moving to another position better support these goals, or are there other ways to improve the current situation?
6. **Support from HR or the works council:** Have you considered contacting the HR department or the works council for support? What options do these internal bodies offer?
7. **Specific expectations for another job:** What do you hope to gain from a change? Is recognition particularly important to you, or are there other aspects (such as workload, leadership style, development opportunities) that could be better in a new job?

This additional information could help to consider the problem more comprehensively and possibly identify alternative solutions before you decide to change jobs.
(Source: ChatGPT 4o; retrieved on 13.08.2024)

The chat thus initiated could be continued by the coachee by informing the chatbot which of its suggestions or questions are useful, and then answering them.

5.2.2 Structuring Available Information

Once the coachee has provided the chatbot with additional information, a conceptually sound next step in the coaching process may be to have the chatbot structure this information. Such an instruction could, for example, be formulated as follows:

User:

Many thanks for the helpful suggestions, which made it clear to me that the following information might also be important:

(So far, there has not actually been a clarifying conversation with the boss, and the reason for this is that I have found the boss does not listen and is hypersensitive to any kind of criticism, immediately interpreting any such remark as a personal attack.) With reference to the information now available, I would like to ask you to tell me according to which criteria it can be meaningfully structured, and then to carry out this structuring.

AI

To structure the available information in a meaningful way, we could divide the problem description into several thematic categories. A possible structure could be as follows:

5

1. **Work environment and previous situation**
   - **Work situation:**Employed as an IT expert for three years in a group with ten colleagues.
   - **Team dynamics:**Good relationship with colleagues and enjoyment of the work.
   - **Feedback culture of previous supervisors:** It is implied that recognition and criticism were handled differently before the change in management, which contributes to the current dissatisfaction.
2. **New management and its impact**
   - **Introduction of the new manager:** A new manager was appointed one month ago.
   - **Manager's leadership style:** The manager exerts significant pressure, considers good performance a given, and regularly criticizes without showing appreciation.
   - **Team perception:**Not only you, but also other colleagues are experiencing the same issue with the manager.
3. **Communication and potential for conflict**
   - **Lack of clarification meeting:** So far, there has been no clarification meeting with the manager, as experience shows that he does not listen.
   - **Assessment of the manager:** The manager is hypersensitive to criticism and interprets it as a personal attack.
4. **Options for action and considerations**
   - **Change of workplace:** Considering looking for a new job either within or outside the company.
   - **Long-term goals and aspirations:** The consideration of a change is based on the desire for a better work environment and possibly more recognition.

This structuring allows for a systematic analysis of the situation and the development of targeted solutions for each category. For example, in the category "Communication and potential for conflict," one could consider how to conduct a conversation despite the manager's difficult personality, or whether alternative communication channels (e.g., through a neutral third party) should be considered. In the category "Options for action and considerations," the advantages and disadvantages of changing jobs could be weighed in detail.

(Source: ChatGPT 4o; retrieved on 13.08.2024)

This answer is not necessarily bad. However, it is somewhat noticeable that the chatbot does not possess differentiated, coaching-specific knowledge. This weakness can be compensated for by giving the chatbot a coaching-specific follow-up task. As illustrated below, this could be linked to the concept of the so-called "Seven-Field Model" (Geißler 2022):

User

Based on all the information available, please now create a "structured report of the current and desired situation" written in the first person. In this report, summarize all the information currently available regarding the problem and goal description, and divide it into two parts by first describing the current situation and then the desired situation as I would like it to be. In each of the two parts, refer – as far as possible – to the following aspects:

- *the existing external conditions and external resources, including my physical conditions,*
- *my psychological processes (such as feelings, motivational impulses, and thoughts) that are currently triggered in me by the present coaching issue,*
- *my observable behaviors that are currently triggered in me by the present coaching issue,*
- *and the actual consequences that my observable behaviors cause for those around me and for myself.*

AI

Report on the Current and Target Situation

1. **Current Situation**

External Conditions and External Resources

I have been working as an IT expert in a team with ten colleagues for three years. I generally enjoy my work and have a good relationship with the other team members. However, about a month ago, a new manager was appointed whose leadership style is causing significant problems. He exerts strong pressure, takes good performance for granted, and shows no recognition. Instead, he regularly criticizes that performance is insufficient and needs to be improved. This criticism affects not only me but also my colleagues, leading to general dissatisfaction within the team. Physically, I still feel able to cope with my work, but the ongoing strain caused by the manager's leadership style is starting to increase my stress levels.

Psychological Processes

Due to the constant pressure and lack of recognition, I am feeling increasingly frustrated and demotivated. Although I continue to perform my work well, I get the impression that my efforts are not appreciated, which is emotionally burdensome. The thought of discussing these issues with my manager causes me stress and discomfort, as I have experienced that he is hypersensitive to criticism and perceives any comment as a personal attack. This situation creates an internal conflict for me: on the one hand, I want to resolve the situation, but on the other hand, I am afraid of negative consequences from such a conversation.

5

Observable Behaviors

Because of my negative experiences with the manager, I have so far avoided seeking a conversation with him. Instead, I focus on doing my work as well as possible to avoid giving any grounds for criticism. I withdraw emotionally and try to avoid conflicts by not openly showing my discontent. At the same time, I am increasingly considering leaving the company and looking for another job to escape the stressful situation.

Factual Consequences

My behavior has resulted in the problem remaining unresolved so far. The stress and frustration I feel are negatively affecting my motivation and overall well-being. Avoiding direct communication with the manager means that the situation persists and may even worsen. I also notice that my emotional distance from my colleagues is increasing, as I am less actively involved in team activities. If the situation continues, there is a risk that my work performance will suffer and I will seriously consider changing jobs.

2. **Target Situation**

External Conditions and External Resources

In the desired target situation, I continue to work in a team where I feel comfortable and enjoy my work. Ideally, the relationship with my manager has improved, or I have found a new job where my performance is recognized and valued. The working conditions are such that I feel comfortable both physically and mentally and can pursue my professional goals. My supervisor's leadership style fosters a positive working environment in which performance is rewarded and constructive feedback is provided.

Psychological Processes

In the target situation, I feel motivated and appreciated. I experience a balance between the demands of my work and the recognition I receive for it. This strengthens my self-confidence and increases my job satisfaction. If there is criticism, I deal with it constructively, as it is seen as an opportunity for development and not as a personal attack. My inner restlessness and feelings of frustration have disappeared, and I look to the future with optimism.

Observable Behaviors

In this target situation, I approach challenges openly and confidently. If there are problems, I address them directly without fear of negative consequences. I proactively work on my development and actively contribute to the team to find solutions together. If I decide to change jobs, it is from a position of strength and clarity about my professional goals.

Factual Consequences

Through my change in behavior and the positive external conditions, I experience a significant increase in job satisfaction and motivation. My relationships with colleagues and my supervisor are constructive and characterized by mutual respect. If I remain in my current position, I actively contribute to a better working environment. If I decide to take a new job, I make this decision consciously and am confident that I can achieve my professional and personal goals there.

This structured report on the current and target situation gives me a clear overview of the current issues and the desired changes, serving as a basis for further decisions and possible courses of action.

(Source: ChatGPT 4o; retrieved on 13.08.2024)

5.2.3 Conducting Problem Analyses

After the coachee has received the above output, it is conceptually advisable from a coaching perspective to use a third AI prompt to inquire about the root causes of the problem. As the following example shows, it must be taken into account from the outset that non-coaching-specific chatbots do not possess diagnostic coaching knowledge, but instead tend to present an eclectic conceptual collection of as many reasons as possible that appear somehow plausible.

User

Based on the information just provided, can you tell me what the central causes of my issue are?

AI

Based on the available information, the central causes of your issue can be summarized as follows:

1. **Leadership style of the new manager**
   - **Lack of recognition:** Your new manager takes good performance for granted and does not show appreciation, which leads to frustration and demotivation. However, recognition is an important motivational factor, and its absence negatively impacts morale.
   - **Focus on criticism:** The manager places strong emphasis on criticism and questions employees' performance, which contributes to feelings of insecurity and low self-worth.
2. **Communication problems**
   - **Difficult communication:** You have experienced that the manager reacts hypersensitively to criticism and perceives it as a personal attack. This makes open and constructive communication difficult, as you fear that a conversation could have negative consequences.
   - **Conflict avoidance:** Due to these communication difficulties, you avoid direct conversations, which means the problem remains unresolved and may even worsen.
3. **Psychological and emotional strain**
   - **Internal frustration:** The lack of recognition and constant criticism trigger frustration and decreasing motivation. This emotional strain affects not only your well-being but also your ability to act proactively.
   - **Stress and insecurity:** The work environment, characterized by pressure and criticism, creates elevated stress levels. Uncertainty about your own performance and the lack of opportunity to clarify the situation contribute to this strain.

4. **Lack of alternative courses of action**
   - **Internal blockage:** Although you are aware of the problem, you feel blocked from taking direct action, whether by having a conversation with your manager or actively seeking a new job. This blockage intensifies dissatisfaction and the feeling of powerlessness.
5. **Impact on behavior and relationships**
   - **Withdrawal and isolation:** The emotional strain and avoidance of conflict lead you to withdraw, both emotionally and within the team. This not only affects your own satisfaction but also the dynamics and cohesion of the team.

5

Summary:
The central cause of your issue lies in an unhealthy leadership culture characterized by a lack of recognition, excessive criticism, and a difficult communication environment. These external conditions lead to significant psychological strain, which manifests as frustration, stress, and a tendency to avoid conflict. As a result, you remain trapped in a situation that severely impairs your job satisfaction and well-being.

(Source: ChatGPT 4o; retrieved on 13.08.2024)

5.2.4 Specifying Follow-up Questions

The above answer is not entirely bad. However, it does not meet the standards of professional coaching practice. This is because coaching must be oriented towards addressing the coachee as an agent of action. Therefore, the root cause analysis must focus on those causes that lie within the coachee. Only these are within the coachee's sphere of influence, i.e., only these can be changed by the coachee. This shortcoming can be mitigated by specifying follow-up questions. As the following example illustrates, this, however, requires relatively advanced coaching competencies:

User

Thank you for your answer.
Is it possible that I am unconsciously stabilizing my problem through certain beliefs and actions? What could these be?

AI

Yes, it is quite possible that certain beliefs and actions unconsciously contribute to stabilizing your problem. This is a common phenomenon, where certain patterns of thinking and behavior lead to a difficult situation remaining unchanged. Here are some possible mechanisms that could be at play in your case:

1. **Avoidance of Confrontation**
   - **Belief:**You believe that a clarifying conversation with your manager would go badly, as he perceives criticism as a personal attack. This assumption

could lead you to avoid confrontations in order to escape potential conflicts or uncomfortable situations.
   - **Action:**Out of fear of possible consequences, you avoid seeking a conversation with your manager. As a result, the problem remains unresolved, and the situation stabilizes at an unsatisfactory level.
2. **Perfectionism and High Expectations of Yourself**
   - **Belief:**You may have very high expectations of your own performance and take it for granted that you must always deliver excellent work. This could lead you to perceive the lack of recognition as a personal defeat, even though the problem actually lies more in your manager's leadership style.
   - **Action:**By continuing to work at a high level despite difficult circumstances, without allowing yourself or others the opportunity for reflection or change, you unconsciously stabilize the current situation.
3. **Belief in the Immutability of the Situation**
   - **Belief:**You might unconsciously believe that nothing can be changed about the situation because you assume your manager is incapable of change. This belief can keep you stuck in a passive stance.
   - **Action:**This assumption could lead you not to actively seek solutions, because you believe that all attempts are doomed to fail anyway. In this way, you contribute to the stabilization of the problem.
4. **Lack of Self-Confidence Regarding Change**
   - **Belief:** Perhaps you doubt whether you are capable of bringing about positive change yourself, whether through a clarifying conversation or a job change.
   - **Action:** These doubts could prevent you from taking the necessary steps toward change. By holding back, you stabilize the existing situation, even if it is unsatisfactory.
5. **Fear of the Consequences of Change**
   - **Belief:** The fear of the uncertainties associated with changing jobs, such as whether you will be satisfied in a new position or whether you might encounter similar problems there, could unconsciously contribute to stabilization.
   - **Action:** This fear could lead you to remain in your current, unsatisfactory situation because the known difficulties seem less frightening than the unknown.

Summary:
Through the beliefs and actions mentioned above, you unconsciously contribute to the stabilization of your problem. These patterns of thinking and behavior prevent you from actively taking the steps necessary to improve the situation. Consciously reflecting on these patterns and working specifically to change them could help you break out of the stabilized problem situation and find new solutions.

(Source: ChatGPT 4o; retrieved on 13.08.2024)

5.2.5 Criteria-Based Development of Concepts

Based on this response, it makes sense to prompt the chatbot to develop an appropriate concept based on specific criteria. Creating such a prompt also requires knowledge of coaching concepts, which cannot be assumed for coachees.

5

User

Thank you for the helpful suggestions, which made it clear to me that my perfectionism is playing a role here. Assuming that is correct: What would be a good solution strategy for me?

AI

If perfectionism plays a central role in your issue, then an effective solution strategy could be to consciously question and deliberately reduce this perfectionism. Here are some steps that may help you:

1. **Self-reflection and Awareness**
   - **Recognize perfectionism:** Become aware of the areas in your life or work where you are particularly perfectionistic. Ask yourself where these high standards come from and what goals you are pursuing with them. It can be helpful to consider the advantages and disadvantages of your perfectionism.
   - **Question your standards:** Consider whether the standards you set for yourself are realistic and necessary. Are they perhaps too high? Would lower standards also lead to a good result without putting excessive pressure on yourself?
2. **Set realistic goals**
   - **Prioritize your tasks:** Distinguish between tasks that truly require high precision and those for which "good enough" is sufficient. Set clear priorities and avoid striving for perfection in all areas.
   - **Accept mistakes:**Allow yourself to make mistakes and view them as learning opportunities rather than failures. This can reduce pressure and help you approach tasks more calmly.
3. **Communication and Feedback**
   - **Share your concerns:** Talk to your manager or a trusted colleague about your challenges and how your perfectionism may be affecting your work. It may turn out that others do not expect such high standards from you, which could relieve some of the pressure.
   - **Seek feedback:**Ask your manager or colleagues for constructive feedback to get a realistic assessment of your work. This can help you align your own standards with the actual work environment.
4. **Gradual Reduction of Perfectionism**
   - **Set conscious boundaries:** Work on deliberately not completing tasks to absolute perfection, but rather finishing them as "good enough." Start with less important tasks and gradually increase the challenge.
   - **Reward yourself for progress:** Acknowledge and reward yourself when you manage to complete a task without striving for perfection. This can help establish new, healthier behavioral patterns.

5. **Focus on the Essentials**
   - **Appreciate your own performance:** Try to value your work independently of external benchmarks or perfectionist standards. Remember that not every task has to be perfect to be valuable.
   - **Healthy self-confidence:** Develop a healthy self-confidence that is not solely dependent on your performance. Remind yourself that you are valuable as a person, regardless of your work.
6. **Developing an Open Communication Culture**

   - **Initiate a conversation:** Despite the difficulty in dealing with your manager, it may be helpful to seek a conversation in which you openly discuss expectations and pressure. Focus on finding solutions together rather than expressing criticism.
   - **Cooperative collaboration:** Try to foster a cooperative working style that emphasizes teamwork and mutual support. This can help reduce individual perfectionist pressure.

Summary:
Reducing your perfectionism could involve setting more realistic expectations for yourself, consciously questioning your standards, and finding a balance between performance and well-being. Through gradual changes in your mindset and behavior, you can reduce pressure while improving both the quality of your work and your well-being. This could also lead to better communication with your manager and an overall more positive work situation.

(Source: ChatGPT 4o; retrieved on 13.08.2024)

Unfortunately, this response is not entirely satisfactory. Here, one of the central weaknesses of non-coaching-specific chatbots becomes apparent: their tendency to provide as many different thought-provoking ideas, tips, and pieces of advice as possible. While these are brilliantly formulated, they do not sufficiently take into account the specifics of the case at hand. However, this would in principle have been possible, given the now quite extensive case-specific knowledge at this stage of the coaching process.

As will be shown in ▶ Ch. 8, these weaknesses can only be overcome by programming coaching-specific knowledge into the chatbot, thereby turning it into a coaching AI agent.

5.3 Double-loop AI Prompts

Before the triadic AI coaching with coaching-specific knowledge announced in Ch. 8 is presented and discussed, we will now look at the ways in which the quality of prompt scripts can be optimized by supplementing the single-loop AI prompts presented in the previous section with double-loop AI prompts.

The specific added value of these AI prompts lies in the fact that they illuminate the blind spots of single-loop AI prompts, namely their underlying implicit, i.e., unarticulated and unreflected, assumptions and values. They are therefore a central foundation for *double-loop coaching*.

For this reason, it makes sense to enrich the single-loop AI prompt script used above with double-loop AI prompts. These can consist of instructing the non-coaching-specific chatbot to

- identify the implicit assumptions and values in the problem description provided by the client (i.e., coachees or coaches),
- identify and justify the assumptions and values underlying an AI output that has already been provided,
- and/or identify and justify the assumptions and values that the chatbot would apply to a specific assignment.

5

In contrast to the sequence of single-loop AI prompts, the three double-loop AI prompts just mentioned can be meaningfully inserted at several points in the exemplary prompt script presented above (Fig. 5.4). For example, the double-loop AI prompt that asks for the identification of the assumptions and values implicitly underlying the description of the coaching problem can be given before the first single-loop AI prompt as well as after the first or second single-loop AI prompt.

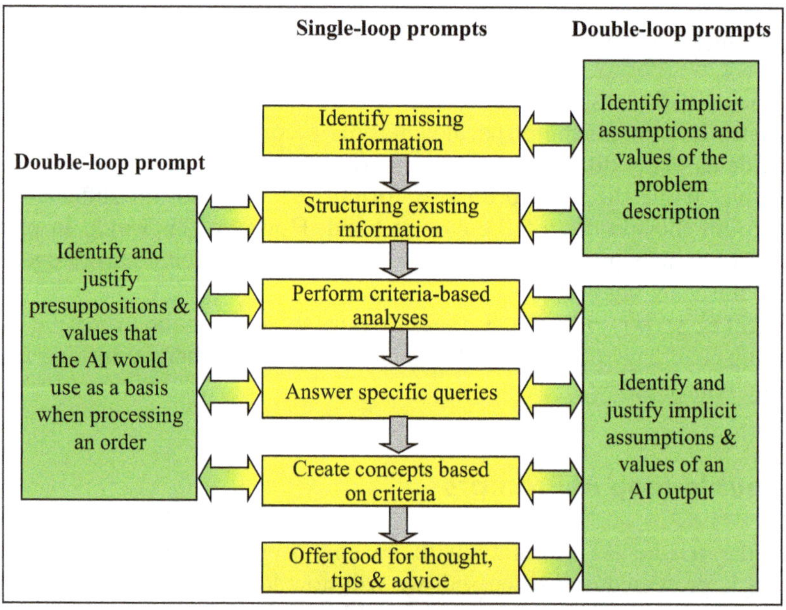

Fig. 5.4 Enriching AI-external single-loop prompts with double-loop prompts

The second double-loop AI prompt, on the other hand, requires the completion of the third or fourth, fifth, or sixth single-loop AI prompt.

Accordingly, the third double-loop AI prompt can only be given after the second or third, fourth and/or fifth single-loop AI prompt.

5.3.1 Having implicit assumptions and values in one's own problem description identified

The three double-loop AI prompts just mentioned are illustrated below using the chat transcript printed in ▶ Sect. 5.3. For the first of these three double-loop AI prompts, this means the following:

User

I have the following problem:

(I have been working as an IT specialist in a group with ten colleagues for three years. I enjoy the work and get along well with the others. My problem is that a month ago we got a boss who only puts pressure on us and takes good performance for granted. Although I continue to deliver good performance, I receive no recognition for it. On the contrary, he repeatedly makes it clear to me that the current performance is not sufficient and must be improved. I am not the only one with this problem; the others feel the same way. Since I assume that I cannot change my boss, my only option is to look for another job, either within the company or elsewhere.)

Analyze the above problem description and tell me which implicit assumptions and values are contained in it.

AI

The problem description contains several implicit assumptions and values that influence the perception and evaluation of the situation. Here are the key assumptions and values:

1. **Implicit assumptions**
   - **The boss cannot be changed:** The assumption that the boss cannot or will not change is strongly implicit. This leads to the possibility of improving the situation through communication or feedback being ruled out from the outset.
   - **Performance should be recognized:** It is assumed that good performance deserves recognition. The lack of recognition is perceived as a problem, indicating that recognition is an important aspect of your work motivation and satisfaction.
   - **Pressure and criticism are negative:** The description suggests that the pressure exerted by the boss and the constant criticism are seen as negative leadership elements that worsen the work situation.
   - **Changing jobs as the last resort:** The assumption that the only way out is to change jobs suggests that you see no other options for improving the situation, such as internal discussions or changes within the team.

2. **Implicit values**
   - **Value of recognition:** The problem description suggests that recognition for work performed is an important value for you. The absence of recognition is perceived as a significant problem, showing that appreciation and respect are central values for your job satisfaction.
   - **Value of performance:** It is implied that performance is highly valued, both in your own perception and in the expectation that this performance will be recognized by others (especially the boss).
   - **Value of job satisfaction:** Your satisfaction at work is a central value that is impaired by the new boss's leadership style. This satisfaction is closely linked to the work climate, recognition, and the type of leadership.
   - **Value of team harmony:** You value good relationships with your colleagues. The fact that you get along well with them and highlight this positively shows that a harmonious team environment is important to you.

Summary:
The problem description contains the assumption that the boss cannot be changed and that the only solution might be to change jobs. At the same time, values such as the importance of recognition, performance, and job satisfaction are evident, which are in conflict with the current situation. These implicit assumptions and values shape the way you perceive the problem and the solution strategies you consider. A more conscious questioning of these assumptions could help to identify new courses of action.

(Source: ChatGPT 4o; retrieved on 13.08.2024)

This answer is impressive. It refers in a differentiated way to the problem description provided and offers valuable food for thought. Even without reference to coaching-specific knowledge, it largely meets the standards of professional coaching.

5.3.2 Identifying and Justifying Implicit Assumptions and Values in AI Output

The same applies to the second double-loop AI prompt, i.e., the task in which the chatbot is asked to identify and justify the implicit assumptions and values underlying its previously provided output.

The following test demonstrates this assessment. It directly follows the chat presented in the previous section, specifically the AI's response to the question regarding the causes of the current issue.

To keep the presentation clear, reference is made not to the entire response, but only to the first of the five possible causes mentioned in that answer:

User

You told me that a central cause of my issue could be the avoidance of conflict. You wrote the following, verbatim:

(Avoidance of confrontation

- *Belief: You believe that a clarifying conversation with your manager would go badly, as he perceives criticism as a personal attack. This assumption may lead you to avoid confrontation in order to escape potential conflicts or uncomfortable situations.*
- *Action: Out of fear of possible consequences, you avoid seeking a conversation with your manager. As a result, the problem remains unresolved, and the situation stabilizes at an unsatisfactory level.)*

I find your analysis interesting and would like to ask you to identify and justify the implicit assumptions and values in this analysis.

AI

The analysis I provided also contains implicit assumptions and values that are worth examining more closely. Here are the key assumptions and values, along with a justification:

Implicit Assumptions

1. **Conflicts are avoidable but problematic:**
   - **Assumption:** It is assumed that you consciously avoid confrontation because you fear negative consequences. This assumption implies that, in your perception, conflicts are seen as potentially harmful or unpleasant, and that you believe you can avoid them without worsening the situation.
   - **Justification:** This assumption is based on the idea that your decision not to seek a conversation with your manager is due to your fear of negative consequences (such as tension or deteriorating working conditions).
2. **Clarifying conversations are risky:**
   - **Assumption:** It is implied that a clarifying conversation with the manager carries a certain risk, particularly based on the assumption that the manager might perceive criticism as a personal attack. This assumption presumes that you have had negative experiences with your manager that have led to this assessment.
   - **Justification:** This assumption arises from your described experience with the manager and the belief that such a conversation could potentially worsen the situation.
3. **Avoidance behavior stabilizes problems:**
   - **Assumption:** The analysis assumes that avoiding confrontation leads to the problem remaining unresolved and the situation stabilizing at an unsatisfactory level. This implies that actively addressing the problem could lead to an improvement in the situation.
   - **Justification:** This assumption is based on the belief that addressing conflicts can lead to solutions, and that inaction often only worsens or entrenches the situation.

Implicit Values

1. **Value of direct communication:**
   - **Value:**The implicit value here is that direct communication, even in difficult situations, is fundamentally positive and necessary to resolve problems.
   - **Justification:**This assumption is based on the idea that an open conversation with the manager could clear up misunderstandings or lead to solutions, indicating a positive evaluation of transparency and direct communication.
2. **Value of self-efficacy:**
   - **Value:**The analysis presupposes that by taking active steps (e.g., having a clarifying conversation), you can improve your situation. This reflects the value of self-efficacy, i.e., the belief that you are able to influence your environment and circumstances through your own actions.
   - **Justification:**This value is evident in the analysis's implication that your actions (or inaction) have a direct impact on stabilizing or resolving the issue.
3. **Value of conflict resolution:**
   - **Value:**It is assumed that dealing with conflicts, rather than avoiding them, leads to better outcomes. This assumption is based on the value of actively engaging with problems and the belief that such engagement is necessary to achieve progress.
   - **Justification:**This value is reflected in the analysis's view that direct confrontation is a potential solution, rather than continuing to avoid the issue.

Summary:

The analysis I have provided contains assumptions that direct communication and conflict resolution are important and necessary to solve problems, and that avoiding confrontation tends to stabilize the problem. These assumptions and values reflect a positive evaluation of openness, self-efficacy, and active problem-solving, implying that these approaches could lead to an improvement in your situation.

(Source: ChatGPT 4o; retrieved on 13.08.2024)

5.3.3 Identifying and Justifying the Assumptions and Values that AI Would Apply when Handling a Specific Task

The positive assessment of the first and second double-loop AI prompts applies without reservation to the third as well.

To test it in practice, the above chat was continued as follows:

User

Thank you. That sounds interesting, and I am considering whether, on this basis, I should assign you the task of telling me what I can do in practical terms in the short term to solve my problem.

Before I give you this task, however, I would first like to know which assumptions and values you would apply to this potential assignment and how you would justify these assumptions and values.

AI

If you assign me the task of suggesting practical short-term solutions, these would also be based on certain assumptions and values. Here are the key assumptions and values, along with a justification:

Implicit Assumptions

1. **Changeability of the Situation:**
   - **Assumption:**It is assumed that the current situation can be changed through targeted actions and decisions. This assumption is based on the idea that you are able to positively influence your work situation through your behavior and decisions.
   - **Justification:**This assumption is based on the belief that people can actively shape their environment and do not have to react passively to external circumstances. By providing practical advice, I assume that you can implement it and that it will have an effect.
2. **Possibility of Short-Term Improvement:**
   - **Assumption:**It is assumed that small but targeted measures can lead to an improvement in the situation in the short term. This assumption is based on the idea that a comprehensive solution is not always immediately necessary, but that small steps can also lead to noticeable relief.
   - **Justification:**This assumption is supported by the insight that change can often be initiated by small, concrete actions, which then trigger a chain reaction of positive developments.
3. **Resource Orientation:**
   - **Assumption:**I would assume that you have certain resources and capabilities that you can use to improve your situation. This assumption implies that you are not "helpless," but already possess tools and skills that you can apply.
   - **Justification:**This assumption is based on the idea that everyone has strengths and resources that can be used in challenging situations. This perspective is resource-oriented and aims to activate your existing competencies.

Implicit Values

1. **Value of Self-Efficacy:**
   - **Value:**A central value underlying this approach is the belief in self-efficacy. This means that you are able to bring about positive change through your own actions.
   - **Justification:**This value is important because it gives you back control over your situation and encourages you to actively seek solutions instead of passively waiting for external changes.
2. **Value of Pragmatism:**
   - **Value:**For short-term solutions, the value of pragmatism would be paramount, meaning the idea that practical, actionable steps are often more effective than theoretical considerations or long-term plans that are harder to implement.

   - **Justification:**This value is central because it focuses on the immediate feasibility and practical benefit of the proposed measures. In challenging situations, it is often more important to do something quickly that has a direct impact.
3. **Value of Positive Change:**
   - **Value:**The underlying value would be the pursuit of positive change and improvement of the current situation, regardless of how small or large that change may be.
   - **Justification:**This value is crucial because it aims to gradually improve quality of life and satisfaction. It emphasizes the importance of progress and development, even if these occur in small steps.

Summary:
If I were to suggest practical short-term solutions, this would be based on the assumptions that you can improve the situation through targeted actions, that short-term measures can be effective, and that you have the necessary resources to do so. The underlying values would be self-efficacy, pragmatism, and the pursuit of positive change. These assumptions and values are intended to provide you with actionable and effective solutions that can be directly applied in your daily life.

(Source: ChatGPT 4o; retrieved on 13.08.2024)

References

Argyris C, Schön D (1978) Organizational learning: a theory of action perspective. Addison-Wesley, Reading/Mass.

Edenhausen (2024) Coaching und Beratung treffen auf KI. Der systemische Ansatz in Zeiten von ChatGPT. Selbstverlag, Innsbruck

Geißler H (2022) Sieben-Felder-Schema. In: Rauen C (Hrsg) Coaching-Tools, 12. Aufl. managerSeminare, Bonn, S 194–199

Non-Coaching-Specific Chatbots and their Coaching-Specific Use Through External AI Prompt Scripts that Connect AI Prompts with Coach Prompts

Contents

H. Geissler, *AI-Coaching*,
https://doi.org/10.1007/978-3-658-49178-9_6

In ▶ Sect. 5.1 it was pointed out that the use of non-coaching-specific chatbots for coaching purposes requires an interaction between users, i.e., coachees or coaches, and the chatbot, in which, in simplified terms, they must perform two tasks, namely

- reflection processes that serve to prepare the prompts they give to the chatbot,
- and reflection processes that relate to engaging with the output produced by the chatbot.

Even if only indirectly, the quality of these reflection processes determines the quality of the AI output. It is therefore advisable to methodically guide the reflection activities of users, i.e., coachees and coaches, in the sense of the *"human-in-the-loop" approach* mentioned in ▶ Sect. 2.2.1, using AI-external prompt scripts, which are characterized by the fact that all AI prompts are prepared and followed up by user prompts. As these prompts, as will become clear below, are relatively demanding from a coaching conceptual perspective, it makes sense that they are directed exclusively at coaches who are attempting to integrate non-coaching-specific chatbots into their dialogues with coachees.

On this basis, i.e., with the help of corresponding instructions for coaches, it becomes possible to combine the use of non-coaching-specific chatbots with other digital coaching tools, including text-based and image-based tools as well as 3D tools that, for example, offer avatars in virtual worlds for constellation work (◘ Fig. 6.1).

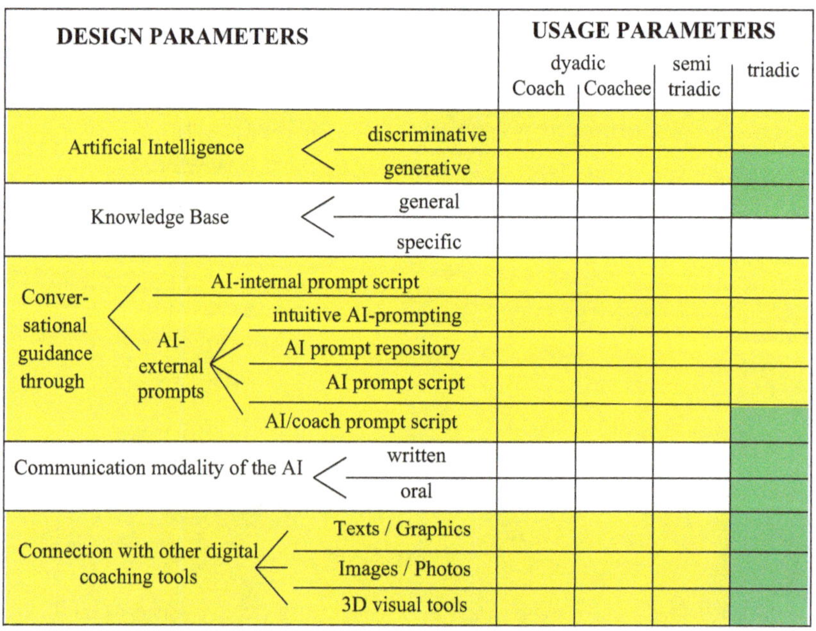

◘ **Fig. 6.1** Coaching-unspecific chatbots and their coaching-specific triadic use through AI-external prompt scripts that connect AI prompts with coach prompts

Chapter 8 will show that these design parameters are also of fundamental importance for the approach of triadic AI coaching with coaching-diagnostic knowledge and an AI-external prompt script.

6.1 The Structure of AI-External Prompt-Clusters

In order to methodically guide the reflection processes that coaches should conduct with their coachees to optimally prepare AI prompts—and not least to ensure that the output of the chatbots is also systematically reflected upon—it is advisable to work with *prompt-clusters* that consist of three parts (Fig. 6.2), namely:

- a prompt directed at the coach, instructing them to adopt a specific methodological behavior in dealing with the coachee, with the aim that this behavior results in the creation of a protocol, the introductory sentence of which is specified in writing by a coach prompt.
- This protocol is then combined with a written, pre-formulated task and sent to the chatbot.
- The output subsequently received from the chatbot can be optimally utilized in the sense of the *"human-in-the-loop" approach* if coach and coachee systematically reflect on it, and the coach is guided and prompted by a corresponding prompt to communicate the result of this reflection to the chatbot in a protocol, thereby providing feedback.

Each of these coach prompts and AI prompts has a specifically targeted effectiveness. This can be captured using the success factors reconstructed by Greif and Behrendt. However, in their previous publications (Behrendt and Greif 2018; Greif 2015, 2021; Greif et al. 2012), these refer only to face-to-face coaching. In order to also take into account the specifics of AI coaching, Siegfried Greif has therefore suggested in discussions with the author to add the transmission of coaching-relevant knowledge as an additional success factor.

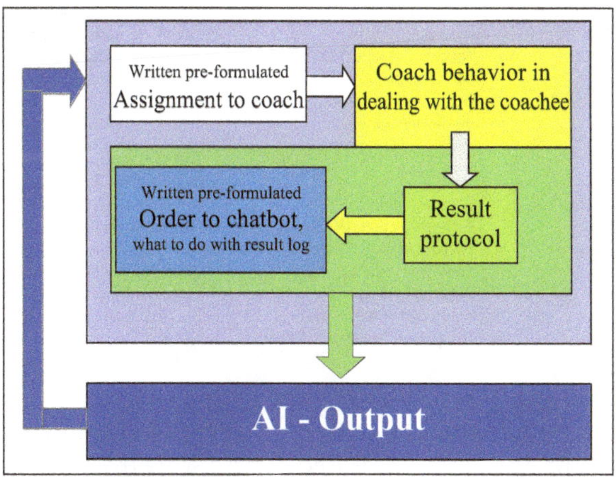

Fig. 6.2 The structure of AI-external prompt-cluster

On this basis, the causal effectiveness of prompts directed at coaches and chatbots can be assessed with reference to the following success factors:

Effect factor	Coach prompt	AI prompt
Process management	The prompt is formulated in such a way that it encourages coaches to structure the coaching process in a specific way on the conceptual basis of process consulting and to assume leadership responsibility for it.	The prompt is formulated in such a way that it encourages the chatbot to produce an output aimed at suggesting a specific structure of the coaching process to coaches and coachees on the conceptual basis of process consulting.
Knowledge transfer	The prompt is formulated in such a way that it encourages coaches to impart knowledge to their coachees that is important for their coaching topic.	The prompt is formulated in such a way that it encourages the chatbot to produce an output that provides the coachees with knowledge that is important for their coaching topic.
Emotional support	The prompt is formulated in such a way that it encourages coaches to support their coachees emotionally in a certain way.	The prompt is formulated in such a way that it encourages the chatbot to produce an output that is suitable for supporting the coachees emotionally in a certain way.
Affect regulation	The prompt is formulated in such a way that it encourages coaches to dampen or intensify the emotions of their coachees in a certain way.	The prompt is formulated in such a way that it encourages the chatbot to produce an output that is suitable for dampening or intensifying the affects of the coachees in a certain way.
Goal and will clarification	The prompt is formulated in such a way that it encourages coaches to stimulate and support their coachees to clarify their goals and motivation.	The prompt is formulated in such a way that it encourages the chatbot to produce an output that is suitable for stimulating and supporting the coachees to clarify their goals and motivation.
Problem and self-reflection	The prompt is formulated in such a way that it encourages coaches to stimulate and support their coachees to reflect on their problems and themselves in a certain way.	The prompt is formulated in such a way that it encourages the chatbot to produce an output that is suitable for stimulating and supporting the coachees to reflect on their problems and themselves in a certain way.
Activation of resources	that it encourages coaches to stimulate and support their coachees to perceive and use certain external and psychological resources in a goal-oriented way.	The prompt is formulated in such a way that it encourages the chatbot to produce an output that is suitable for stimulating and supporting the coachees to perceive and use certain external and psychological resources in a goal-oriented manner.
Implementation support	The prompt is formulated in such a way that it encourages coaches to support their coachees in the practical implementation of the developed solution strategy and goal-oriented activities.	The prompt is formulated in such a way that it encourages the chatbot to produce an output that is suitable for supporting the coachees in the practical implementation of the developed solution strategy and goal-oriented activities.

The strength of the effectiveness that results solely from the linguistic formulation of the respective prompt can be measured using a scale from 0 to 4, as follows:

- a "4" indicates a very high effectiveness,
- a "3" indicates high effectiveness,
- a "2" indicates moderately high effectiveness,
- a "1" indicates low effectiveness,
- and a "0" indicates minimal or no effectiveness.

These considerations will be illustrated below with an example relating to the start of a triadic coaching process in which coach and coachee use ChatGPT as a coaching tool. This example closely resembles the example used in ▶ Sect. 8.3 to illustrate triadic AI coaching with coaching-diagnostic knowledge and a prompt script.

The first prompt-cluster analyzed below consists of three individual prompts, the first two of which are addressed to the coach and the third to the chatbot. In this way, the coaching process is guided as follows:

- The coach greets the coachee and then shares the screen to introduce the concept and procedure of AI coaching. In doing so, the coach pays particular attention to building a positive working relationship.
- Next, the coach addresses the coaching issue and encourages the coachee to talk about what is troubling them and what they wish for.
- In parallel or with a slight time delay, the coach copies the following text into the non-coaching-specific chatbot:
  "I have the following problem: [...]"
- While the coachee presents their issue, the coach records the key points.
- Afterwards, the coach explains to the coachee that they must review and approve the protocol created in this way, and discusses with them the task to be given to the chatbot in this context.
- On this basis, the coach sends the protocol together with the task to the chatbot.

The rating of this prompt-cluster can be carried out using artificial intelligence, for example by providing ChatGPT with the definition of the success factors and the assessment procedure, and instructing it to assess the effectiveness of each prompt provided with reference to each of the eight success factors, substantiating this assessment with statements from the prompt. To check the quality of these ratings, a follow-up instruction can be given to state the reasons why a higher or lower value was not chosen and, in the spirit of the *"human-in-the-loop" approach*, to decide on this basis whether and to what extent to follow the AI's rating.

In this sense, the following dialogue with ChatGPT took place on 21.10.2024:

User

Determine the effectiveness of the following prompt, which is addressed to the coach: (Coach greets coachee, engages in some small talk, and then shares the screen to introduce the concept and procedure of AI coaching to the coachee. The coach pays particular attention to building a positive working relationship. In this context, the coach checks how much "technically undisturbed" space the coachee needs for presen-

ting their issue—or how helpful it is likely to be to record the presentation of the issue in parallel.)

AI

The effectiveness of the present prompt can be evaluated based on the 8 dimensions:

- Process management:
  The prompt is clearly structured and provides the coach with instructions for managing the process, particularly through the introduction to the concept of AI coaching and consideration of the space the coachee needs to present their issue. This implies a moderate to high level of effectiveness.
  Rating: 3
- Knowledge transfer:
  The prompt stipulates that the coach explains the concept and procedure of AI coaching to the coachee. This implies active knowledge transfer, but without going into detail about the method of delivery. Therefore, the effectiveness is moderate.
  Rating: 2
- Emotional support:
  The instruction that the coach should build a positive working relationship implies a certain degree of emotional support. However, the support is not explicitly or thoroughly elaborated here.
  Rating: 2
- Affect regulation:
  Affect regulation is not explicitly mentioned in this prompt. There is no direct indication of how the coach should respond to the coachee's emotional reactions.
  Rating: 0
- Goal or will clarification:
  The prompt focuses on presenting the concept and the issue, but not directly on clarifying the coachee's goals or will.
  Rating: 1
- Problem and self-reflection:
  The coach is expected to check how the coachee presents their issue. This suggests a moderate promotion of issue presentation and reflection.
  Rating: 2
- Resource activation:
  Resource activation is implicit here through the focus on presenting the issue and enabling an undisturbed space, but is not explicitly promoted.
  Rating: 1
- Implementation support:
  The prompt does not contain explicit instructions on how the coach should support the practical implementation of the discussed content.
  Rating: 0

User

You rate process management as "3". What speaks against a "4"?

AI

The rating of "3" instead of "4" in **process management** is due to the fact that, while the prompt provides a clear structure (greeting, small talk, introduction to AI coaching, checking the need for space to present the issue), it does not contain particularly detailed or explicit instructions for managing the entire coaching process. The coach is guided to a certain extent in their leadership responsibility, but there are no indications of further steps or specific techniques to continuously and precisely guide the process beyond this initial phase.

This last statement is thought-provoking, but not entirely convincing, because a management of the coaching process that ChatGPT would rate as a "4" would not be optimal with regard to the concept of process consulting.

Table 6.1 Assessment of the effectiveness of prompts in triadic AI coaching

Prompt	Effectiveness Rating
'Coach greets the coaching partner, engages in some small talk, and then shares the screen to introduce the coachee to the concept and process of AI coaching. The coach pays particular attention to building a positive working relationship. In this context, the coach checks how much "media-technically undisturbed" space the coachee needs to present their issue—or how helpful it might be to document the presentation of the issue in parallel.'	4 Process Management 2 Knowledge Transfer 2 Emotional Support 0 Affect Regulation 1 Goal or Will Clarification 2 Problem and Self-Reflection 1 Resource Activation 0 Implementation Support
'Coach encourages the coachee to describe the current unsatisfactory ACTUAL situation and how they envision the DESIRED situation. The coach limits themselves to active listening.'	3 Process Management 0 Knowledge Transfer 3 Emotional Support 1 Affect Regulation 2 Goal or Will Clarification 4 Problem and Self-Reflection 0 Resource Activation 0 Implementation Support
I have the following problem or coaching goal: [Coach empathetically documents the coachee's statements regarding the current ACTUAL situation and the DESIRED situation, and transmits these to the AI agent.]	3 Process Management 0 Knowledge Transfer 3 Emotional Support 1 Affect Regulation 2 Goal or Will Clarification 3 Problem and Self-Reflection 0 Resource Activation 0 Implementation Support
Can you tell me which information that might still be important for the current ACTUAL situation and the DESIRED situation is missing so far, so that I can provide it to you?	2 Process Management 4 Knowledge Transfer 0 Emotional Support 0 Affect Regulation 2 Goal or Will Clarification 2 Problem and Self-Reflection 0 Resource Activation 0 Implementation Support

As illustrated in the following table (Table 6.1), the prompts of the first prompt-cluster of a prompt script (not further detailed here) can be rated as follows with the support of ChatGPT—and after critical reflection on ChatGPT's suggestions:

6.2 Integration with Other Digital Coaching Tools

6

Prompt scripts that systematically connect AI prompts with coach prompts make it possible to link non-coaching-specific chatbots with other digital coaching tools, in particular

- with 2D visual coaching tools that combine graphical or drawing and textual elements,
- with digital images/photos,
- and with 3D visual virtual worlds with avatars.

These possibilities are another important feature of triadic AI coaching, which is presented and discussed in Chapter 8.

6.2.1 Connection with Textual-Graphic Coaching Tool

AI coaching sessions that use a non-coaching-specific chatbot, supported by prompt scripts in which the AI prompts are prepared by coach prompts, are well suited for integration with digital textual-graphic coaching tools. The following will illustrate what needs to be considered in this context, using a coaching tool that helps coachees assess both the actual and desired importance of the life domains or aspects that shape their lives and are important to them. This tool, which can be used in both digital and analog formats, is known as the "Wheel of Life" (Stöger 2020), "Values Wheel," or "Perspectives Wheel" (Geißler and Rödel 2023, p. 205).

To work with this coaching tool, the first step is to identify, together with the coachees, the life domains that are important to them. The result might look as follows:

- Career & Profession
- Relationships with friends, acquaintances, and colleagues
- Health & Fitness
- Family
- Personal Development
- Spirituality
- Well-being

For each of these dimensions, coachees must then assess both the actual and desired importance using a scale from 0 to 10.

This assessment can be reviewed by a chatbot by specifying the single-loop AI prompt for criteria-based analysis and instructing the chatbot to analyze the provided and, if necessary, expanded problem description in terms of how important the various dimensions appear in this description.

User

I have the following problem:

(I have been working as an IT specialist in a group with ten colleagues for three years. I enjoy the work and get along well with the others. My problem is that a month ago we got a new boss who only puts pressure on us and takes good performance for granted. Although I continue to perform well, I receive no recognition for it. This is weighing on me. I can no longer sleep well, and my wife is also putting pressure on me to do something about it.)

Analyze this problem description with regard to the following dimensions and tell me, using a number between 0 and 10, how important the following dimensions are for my problem:

- *Career & Profession*
- *Relationships with friends, acquaintances, and colleagues*
- *Health & Fitness*
- *Family*
- *Personal Development*
- *Spirituality*
- *Well-being*

AI

Here is the analysis of your problem based on the specified dimensions and an assessment of their respective importance:

1. **Career & Profession** (10/10): This is the central aspect of the problem. The change in the work environment due to the new boss and the lack of recognition are at the core of the conflict, leading to dissatisfaction and stress.
2. **Relationships with friends, acquaintances, and colleagues** (7/10): Although you have good relationships with your colleagues, the relationship with your boss plays a decisive role in the professional context. The pressure from your boss also indirectly affects the team dynamic.
3. **Health & Fitness** (8/10): Your sleep problems and the associated stress indicate that the problem is having a significant impact on your health.
4. **Family** (9/10): Your wife is also putting pressure on you, which strongly influences the family dimension. The family pressure increases the urgency to find a solution.
5. **Personal Development** (6/10): The lack of recognition could create the feeling that you are stagnating in your personal growth and professional development. It could be an impetus to reassess professional or personal goals.
6. **Spirituality** (3/10): This does not appear to be a central point in your problem description, but it could be helpful in reflection and coping, depending on how important this aspect is to you in your life in general.
7. **Well-being** (8/10): Your overall well-being is impaired by work-related stress and family strain. It seems this is a significant burden that is affecting your overall sense of life satisfaction.

The problem primarily concerns your professional situation and personal well-being, with a strong impact on your health and family.

(Source: ChatGPT4; retrieved on 24.05.2024)

This response can then be compared and discussed with the coachee's previously created assessment.

6.2.2 Connection with Immersive Image Work

AI coaching sessions that use a non-coaching-specific chatbot, supported by prompt scripts in which the AI prompts are prepared by coach prompts, are also well suited for conducting immersive image work (Messerschmidt 2015; Geißler and Rödel 2023).

For this, coaches need to show their coachees a series of emotionally impactful images/photos and ask them to select the image that best represents a particular aspect or the entirety of their issue. They then encourage and support the coachees in mentally immersing themselves in this image and intensely reliving what they see.

The next step is to explore what substantive connections might exist between the image or the experience just had and the previously discussed coaching issue.

Afterwards the coach shows the AI this image and inform it that a coachee has selected this image to visualize their coaching issue. Based on this contextual information, the question is then posed as to what important characteristics and possible causes of this issue might be.

This task can lead to the following result:

AI

The image selected by the coachee shows a person standing alone in a dense, fog-shrouded forest. It is characterized by a gloomy, mystical atmosphere that may reflect the coachee's emotional states or inner conflicts. Here are some possible characteristics and causes of the issue that could be visualized by the image:

Key characteristics:

1. **Isolation and loneliness:** The coachee is standing alone in a dense forest. This could indicate feelings of loneliness, isolation, or a sense of being cut off from the outside world.
2. **Confusion or disorientation:** The fog that limits visibility could symbolize that the coachee feels unable to see the way forward clearly or is having difficulty making decisions. The fog could also point to uncertainties or ambiguities that are weighing on the coachee.
3. **Feeling of oppression:** The atmosphere of the image is rather gloomy and oppressive, which could indicate a sense of oppression, anxiety, or inner restlessness. The forest can be seen as a symbol for a challenge or problem that the coachee perceives as overwhelming.
4. **Stagnation or inability to act:** The coachee is standing still in an otherwise empty but densely overgrown environment. This could indicate a feeling of being stuck or unable to act, where the coachee does not know how to move forward.

Possible causes:

1. **Unclear life goals or decisions:** The fog and dense forest could point to unclear or undefined goals, making it difficult for the coachee to make decisions or move forward.
2. **Feeling of isolation in personal or professional relationships:** The loneliness in the image could indicate that the coachee feels alienated from others, whether in a personal or professional context.
3. **Fear of the unknown:** The foggy forest could also be a symbol for fear of the unknown or of change. The coachee may have difficulty facing new situations or stepping out of their comfort zone.
4. **Emotional overwhelm:** The gloomy atmosphere could indicate emotional overwhelm or depressive states, in which the coachee feels there is no way out of their situation.

Overall, the image points to a complex emotional or psychological issue that may be associated with feelings of loneliness, disorientation, and anxiety. Further discussion with the coachee about their associations with this image could provide deeper insights into their specific challenges and needs.

(Source: ChatGPT4; retrieved on 24.05.2024)

This AI output can be compared with the coachee's self-interpretation and lead to valuable insights.

The alternative is to mentally put yourself in the coachee's position and write the following prompt:

User

I have the following problem:

(I have been working as an IT specialist in a group with ten colleagues for three years. I enjoy the work and get along well with the others. My problem is that a month ago we got a new boss who only puts pressure on us and takes good performance for granted. Although I continue to deliver good results, I receive no recognition for them. On the contrary, he repeatedly makes it clear that the current performance is not sufficient and must be improved. I am not the only one with this problem; the others feel the same way. Since I assume that I cannot change my boss, my only option is to look for another job, either within the company or elsewhere.)

For this coaching issue, I have selected a suitable image, which I describe as follows: (I chose the image because it accurately describes the mood I have been experiencing more and more often lately. In the image, I see a person who is not clearly recognizable in the fog. When I immerse myself in the image, I feel the deep disorientation and discouragement of this person. My gaze is drawn especially to the indistinct face of this person, and I hear the words inside me: "It just can't be this way!")

My request to you is to establish an internal connection between the coaching issue described above and this image.

The answer with which ChatGPT responds to this prompt is as follows:

AI

The internal connection between your described coaching issue and the image you have selected can be established on several levels.

1. **Feeling of disorientation and discouragement:** The image shows a person who is not clearly recognizable in the fog, which symbolically represents the feeling of disorientation. This feeling corresponds to the situation you are in. You have worked for years in a stable and positive work environment, but since the arrival of the new boss, the atmosphere has changed dramatically. The lack of recognition and constant pressure have led you to feel insecure and disoriented in your role and your value within the team. The fog symbolizes this uncertainty and discomfort that you experience due to the new demands and lack of feedback.
2. **Uncertainty and lack of perspective:** The indistinct face in the image represents the uncertainty about your future professional direction. Just like the person in the fog who cannot see a clear path ahead, you are faced with the decision of whether to remain in your current position or look for new opportunities—either within or outside the company. This uncertainty leads to an inner conflict, as you are not sure which path is right and what consequences your decision might have.
3. **Inner protest against the situation:** The words "It just can't be this way!" reflect your inner resistance and discomfort triggered by the current situation. These words express your dissatisfaction and the feeling that the current circumstances, especially the behavior of the new boss, are unfair and unacceptable. This inner rebellion is a sign that you are longing for change and no longer want to accept the current situation.
4. **The search for clarity and a way out:** The image in the fog could also be interpreted as a metaphor for your search for clarity and a way out of the current situation. The fog stands for the confusion and challenges that stand in your way as you try to make a decision. The fact that the person in the image is standing in the fog could indicate that the way out of the current situation is not easy to see and that it will take time and self-reflection to make a clear decision.

In summary:

The image embodies your emotional and psychological state in this difficult situation. It reflects the uncertainty, lack of recognition, and disorientation brought about by the new boss and the changed work atmosphere. At the same time, the image suggests that you are in a process of self-discovery, trying to find a way out of the fog—towards a clearer and more fulfilling professional future.

(Source: ChatGPT; retrieved on 24.05.2024)

6.2.3 Connection with Constellation Work Using Avatars in Virtual Worlds

Constellation work can be conducted in very different forms and based on various concepts. One possibility is to orient oneself to the concept of the Inner Team (Schulz von Thun 1998).

With regard to the coaching issue that has repeatedly been used as an example in the previous sections, this could mean that the coach and coachee come to the conclusion that the problem is primarily determined by the following two personality parts: on the one hand, the "anxious need-for-approval" part, and on the other, the "defiant fighter."

These two personality parts are visualized in a virtual world using appropriately designed and positioned avatars (Tawadros et al. 2018).

In the next step, the coach suggests conducting an interview with both personality parts, focusing on the question of the coaching goal. An audio recording of this interview is made as the basis for the following transcript:

> "Coach: Hello, both of you. I'm glad to meet you here. I would like to conduct an interview with both of you. I would like to know what ideas you have regarding the current situation, how things should proceed, and in particular, what goal you consider meaningful. Would that be okay for you?
> Coachee: Yes, totally fine.
> Coach: Then I'll start by asking the anxious need-for-approval part. Hello, anxious need-for-approval, how do you see things?
> Coachee: Well, what can I say? It's all really terrible—and I really don't know how things should go on. But maybe the supervisor will change. You should never give up hope.
> Coach: Yes, I understand. And now to you, defiant fighter. Do you see it the same way?
> Coachee: No, of course not. Waiting is completely wrong. That only makes things worse. Because then the supervisor thinks everything can just continue as it is. But it can't. That's why we have to fight. We simply can't put up with it anymore.
> Coach: And what do you suggest?
> Coachee: Work to rule. Especially if the supervisor starts to rage.
> Coach: Okay, understood. And what do you think about that, anxious need-for-approval?
> Coachee: That's absolutely out of the question. That's far too dangerous. I won't go along with that."

Together with the initial problem description from the coachee, this transcript is given to the chatbot with the task of identifying possible underlying causes for the present issue.

This task leads to the following output:

AI

The interview you conducted highlights the internal conflicts that have arisen due to the difficult situation with the new supervisor. To analyze the underlying causes of the described issue, several psychological and organizational aspects can be considered:

1. **Internal Parts and Personality Conflicts**

The interview reveals two different internal parts of the coachee: the "anxious need-for-approval" and the "defiant fighter." These parts represent different coping strategies and attitudes toward the pressure and lack of recognition from the new supervisor.

- **The anxious need-for-approval:** This part is characterized by strong insecurity and a need for recognition. It fears the consequences of standing up to the supervisor. Behind this may lie a deeply rooted need for social acceptance and security, possibly shaped by earlier experiences in which the consequences of confrontation were negative. This part avoids conflict and hopes for an external solution by relying on a change in the supervisor.
- **The defiant fighter:** In contrast, this part is willing to actively fight against the grievances and takes a combative stance. It sees the danger in passively accepting the situation, as this could further encourage the supervisor to exert pressure. This part may stem from a strong sense of justice or a need for autonomy, possibly shaped by earlier experiences in which active intervention led to positive outcomes.

2. **Organizational Dynamics and Power Structures**

The situation also reflects a deeper issue in the power structure and organizational culture. The new supervisor relies on pressure and increased performance without showing recognition, which indicates an authoritarian leadership culture.

- **Lack of recognition:** The absence of praise and constant criticism may point to a leadership culture based on pressure and control rather than motivation and trust. In the long term, this could poison the working climate and lead to employee demotivation.
- **Psychological safety:** The different reactions of the internal parts also show an uncertainty within the team as to whether it is safe to stand up to the supervisor. A lack of psychological safety in the organization could lead employees to avoid expressing their opinions openly or to refrain from resisting practices they perceive as unfair.

3. **Possible Causes and Backgrounds**

The underlying causes of this issue may therefore lie both in the individual personality of the coachee and in the structural and cultural conditions of the organization:

- **Personal imprints and previous experiences:** The two internal parts may have developed from the coachee's earlier experiences and imprints, each of which has developed different coping strategies for dealing with pressure and authority.
- **Leadership culture and power relations:** The authoritarian and high-pressure leadership of the new supervisor may be an expression of a larger problem in the organizational culture, where performance is valued above all else and human needs such as recognition and security are neglected.

4. **Conclusion**

The interview illustrates an internal conflict between the fear of the consequences of confrontation and the need to stand up against unfair treatment. The underlying causes may be found both in the coachee's personal imprints and in the organizational culture. Changing the situation may require both an individual and an organizational engagement with these issues in order to enable a healthy and productive approach to the new leadership situation.

(Source: ChatGPT4; retrieved on 24.05.2024)

References

Behrendt P, Greif S (2018) Erfolgsfaktorem im Coaching-Prozess. In: Greif S, Möller H, Scholl W (Hrsg) Handbuch Schlüsselkonzepte im Coaching. Springer, Wiesbaden, S 163–172

Geißler H, Rödel S (2023) Praxishandbuch professionelles Online-Coaching. Beltz, Weinheim/Basel

Greif S (2015) Allgemeine Wirkfaktoren im Coaching-Prozess. Verhaltensbeobachtungen mit einem Ratingverfahren. In: Geißler H, Wegener R (Hrsg) Bewertung von Coaching-Prozessen. Springer, Wiesbaden, S 51–80

Greif S (2021) Was ist Coaching? Wissenschaftliche Grundlagen und praktische Methoden. S. Greif, Osnabrück

Greif S, Schmidt R, Thamm A (2012) Warum und wodurch Coaching wirkt. Ein Überblick zum Stand der Theorieentwicklung und Forschung über Wirkfaktoren. Z Organisationsberat, Superv, Coach 19(4):75–90

Messerschmidt J (2015) Das Selbst im Bild. Peter Lang, Frankfurt am Main

Schulz von Thun F (1998) Miteinander reden – 3 – Das ‚Innere Team' und situationsgerechte Kommunikation. rororo, Reinbek bei Hamburg

Stöger J (2020) Lebensrad. In: Rauen C (Hrsg) Coaching-Tools, 11. Aufl. managerSeminare, Bonn, S 153–155

Tawadros T, Tinker D, Jackson A (2018) Coaching in a virtual world – Your avatar will see you now. In: Heller J, Triebel C, Hauser B, Koch A (Hrsg) Digitale Medien im Coaching. Springer, Wiesbaden, S 129–137

Coaching-Specific AI Agents with Conversational Competence but Without Coaching Diagnostic Knowledge

Contents

H. Geissler, *AI-Coaching*,
https://doi.org/10.1007/978-3-658-49178-9_7

7.1 Coaching-Specific AI Agents with Generative AI

The AI agents discussed in this section (◘ Fig. 7.1) are characterized by the following features:

- they have been developed on the basis of *generative AI,*
- and their knowledge base is determined, on the one hand, by the general knowledge of the respective *general LLMs* used.
- On the other hand, they also possess *coaching-methodological process design capabilities* that are programmed using *AI-internal prompt scripts.*
- On this basis, it is possible to have
  - *oral*
  - or *written* communication,
- which can be connected to other digital coaching tools, specifically
  - with texts and graphics,
  - images or photos,
  - and with 3D visual animations.

AI agents designed in this way can be used *dyadically,* both by individuals facing a coaching issue and by coaches who are preparing for the next coaching session and want to better understand their coachees' issues and possible solutions (Mai and Rutschmann 2023b, p. 120 f.). If, in addition, one wishes to benefit—at least in part—from the advantages of the "human-in-the-loop" solution approach mentioned in ▶ Sect. 2.2.1, a *semi-triadic* use is recommended instead of the dy-

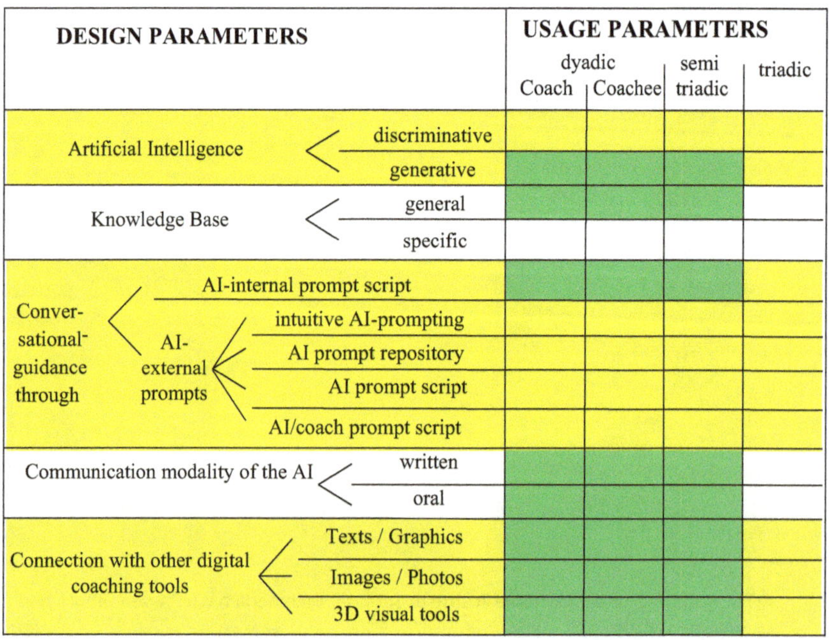

◘ **Fig. 7.1** Coaching AI agents with generative AI and AI-internal prompt scripts, usable in dyadic and semi-triadic settings

adic approach. In this case, coachees use coaching-specific AI agents to prepare for subsequent coaching sessions, in which they discuss the insights and experiences from their dyadic AI coaching with their coaches.

Based on the overview compiled by Rebecca Rutschmann in October 2024 (2024), the following coaching AI agents currently meet the above criteria:

- AICoach Chat (▸ https://www.linkedin.com/company/aicoach-chat/)
- AIMY (▸ https://www.linkedin.com/company/coachhub/)
- Alpina (▸ https://www.linkedin.com/company/evoach/) (May and Rutschmann 2023a, b; Rutschmann 2024)
- Bestselfy (▸ https://www.linkedin.com/company/bestselfy/)
- Bunchee (▸ https://www.linkedin.com/company/bunchai/)
- Coachbot (▸ https://www.linkedin.com/company/coachbot-ai/)
- CoachM (▸ https://www.linkedin.com/company/levertransferoflearning/)
- Lum.Ia and Jul.Ia (▸ https://www.linkedin.com/company/luminous-ai-coaching-platform/)
- Nadia (▸ https://www.linkedin.com/pulse/ai-coaching-next-generation-part2-rebecca-rutschmann-pqgje/)
- PocketConfidant AI (▸ https://pocketconfidant.com/) (Malafronte 2024)
- Rocky AI (▸ https://www.linkedin.com/company/rocky-ai/) (Novic 2024)
- Rypple (▸ https://www.rypple.ai/)
- Sherlock (▸ https://sherlocksupercoach.ai/)
- Vici (Terblanche 2020, 2024a, b)

In addition, there are the AI Business Buddys currently being developed by Oliver Wünsch (▸ https://www.business-buddy.ai/).

One of the biggest problems with these AI agents is data security. However, Rutschmann assesses this as relatively positive, with the exception of two cases (Sherlock and Rypple).

The key difference compared to the use of non-coaching-specific chatbots is that here the AI is controlled by *AI-internal prompt scripts* and not—as described in Chapters 5 and 6—by AI-external prompt scripts. This means that the coaching AI agents manage the *conversation,* not the coachees.

As the following quote from Mai & Rutschmann (2023a, p. 4) illustrates, this requires reference to coaching theories that recommend *clearly structured standardized process steps,* based on the paradigm of *single-loop coaching:*

Single-loop Coaching

"Systemic and solution-oriented coaching models and methods often follow structured and standardized process steps. An intelligent and well-designed coaching chatbot can guide coachees step by step along a decision tree structure. The coaching chatbot only needs to be equipped with the right questions for each process step. The interaction is enriched with visualized and gamified coaching methods and tools, such as the Wheel of Life, constellation boards, techniques from nonviolent communication, or various scaling questions. These can then be integrated into the coaching process depending on the coachee's topic".

How does all this work in practice? – To answer this question, I conducted an experiment on 21.08.2024, in which I put myself in the shoes of a fictional coachee and told “Alpina” the following:

User

I have the following problem:
I have been working as an IT expert in a group with ten colleagues for three years. I enjoy the work and get along well with the others. My problem is that a month ago we got a new boss who only puts pressure on us and takes good performance for granted. Although I continue to deliver good results, I receive no recognition for it. On the contrary, he keeps making it clear to me that my current performance is not sufficient and must be improved. I am not the only one with this problem; the others feel the same way. Since I assume that I cannot change my boss, my only option is to look for another job, either within the company or elsewhere.
Please check whether any important information might be missing from the above problem description and tell me what that could be.

Based on this, the following dialogue developed:

AI

Thank you for your detailed description of your problem. It seems that you and your colleagues are facing a challenge with the new boss, as he has high expectations and gives no recognition for good performance. You are now considering looking for a new job, either within the company or elsewhere.

An important question that comes to mind regarding your situation is: How has this lack of recognition and the pressure from your boss affected your well-being and motivation?

User

Bad. I no longer really enjoy the work. It's no wonder, if you get no recognition, only pressure.

AI

I understand that you feel bad under these conditions.

My next question is: How would you feel if your boss gave you more recognition and put less pressure on you?

User

I would feel better then. It would be like it used to be. Work would be fun and everything would come more easily to me.

AI

I understand, it sounds like recognition for your good work and less pressure from your boss would help you feel better and enjoy your work again.

Another question I would ask is: Are there moments or situations in which you have already had positive experiences regarding recognition and support from your boss or other supervisors?

User
No, things have only gotten worse lately.

AI
I see, so it seems that you have not had any positive experiences regarding recognition and support from your boss or other supervisors recently.

Another question that comes to mind is: Is there anything you could do yourself to feel a bit better in your current situation or to reduce the pressure from your boss?

User
The only thing I can think of is to change jobs—either within the company or to another company. As I said at the beginning.

AI
Yes, you have already mentioned that you are considering looking for another job, either within your current company or elsewhere. Changing jobs could indeed be a way to find yourself in an environment where you receive more recognition and experience less pressure.

Another question I would ask is: What are your personal strengths and skills that could help you in your search for a new job?

User
I am a sought-after IT expert. People like me are in demand everywhere.

AI
That sounds great, that you are in high demand as an IT expert. Your expertise and skills can certainly help you in your search for a new job.

Another question I would ask is: What steps could you take to actively look for a new job?

This chat history shows that each statement by the AI agent consists of two parts: first, the content of the coachee's most recent statement is paraphrased appreciatively and often quite empathetically, and then a follow-up question is asked, the content of which is obviously determined by the programmed prompt script.

In this context, a problem arises that can be summarized as a *fit problem:*
- Because the questions asked do not always directly relate to the content of the paraphrasing
- and the coaching AI agent refuses to process the task that the coachee gives at the beginning of the dialogue.

Conversely, the Alpina chatbot displays a degree of coaching-specific knowledge. This, however, is limited to the paradigm of purposive-rational single-loop coaching outlined in ▶ Chap. 5 and 6. Because

- the coachee's objective of receiving support in finding a new job is adopted *without reflection*
- and the coachee's attention is not directed to questions of meaning, but primarily to existing and potential resources.

To verify this assessment, I shared the above chat history with ChatGPT, along with the information that it was a dialogue between myself as coachee and an AI agent. On this basis, I instructed ChatGPT to reconstruct the program that determines the AI agent's conversational approach. – Here is the response I received:

AI

The dialogue between you and the AI agent can be analyzed from a professional coaching perspective. Here are the positive and less effective aspects of the dialogue:

Positive aspects:

7

1. **Active listening and demonstrating understanding:**
   - The AI agent demonstrates, through repeated paraphrasing and clarifying questions, that it can understand the coachee's problem and emotions. This is a fundamental aspect of coaching to ensure that the coachee feels heard and understood.
2. **Encouragement of self-reflection:**
   - The AI agent asks questions that prompt the coachee to reflect on their situation, feelings, and possible solutions. This fosters self-reflection, which is an essential component of effective coaching.
3. **Identification of resources and strengths:**
   - The AI agent encourages the coachee to recognize and articulate their strengths (e.g., being in demand as an IT expert). This helps the coachee build confidence in their abilities, which is important when seeking solutions or new paths.

Less effective aspects:

1. **Lack of depth and analysis:**
   - The AI agent remains at a rather superficial level and does not delve deeper into the underlying causes of the problem. A professional coach might have asked questions to better understand the dynamics with the new manager and to explore possible internal courses of action.
2. **Lack of concrete action strategies:**
   - The AI agent does not provide specific recommendations or strategies for dealing with the current situation, apart from confirming that changing jobs is an option. A professional coach might have offered suggestions for improving the situation in the current workplace or for systematically searching for new job opportunities.

3. **One-sided focus on changing jobs:**
   - The AI agent picks up on the idea of changing jobs without exploring other potential solutions or approaches. An experienced coach might have discussed alternative strategies, such as communication strategies with the manager, stress management, or networking within the company.
4. **Lack of exploration of alternatives:**
   - No alternative courses of action (other than changing jobs) are discussed. A professional coach would have tried to identify other potential measures that could help the coachee improve the current situation.

Summary:
The dialogue demonstrates some positive aspects, such as active listening and fostering self-reflection. However, the AI agent falls short in terms of depth and the development of concrete solutions or action strategies. A professional coach would have placed greater emphasis on in-depth analysis of the problem, the development of alternatives, and the definition of concrete goals. The AI agent failed to explore the coachee's potential to possibly change the situation and focused too much on changing jobs as the primary solution.

(Source: ChatGPT 4o, retrieved on 21.08.2024)

This assessment raises the question of whether, and to what extent, the identified quality deficiencies can be remedied by improving the AI's internal prompt scripts—or whether the use of internal AI prompt scripts is, above all, a conceptual dead end due to the potentially unsolvable problem of fit, and we need to look for a completely different solution.

To answer this question, I conducted a small experiment on 21.08.2024. The experiment consisted of giving ChatGPT a coaching assignment and presenting it with the same coaching problem as in the above experiment with Alpina, but without instructing it to first list all missing information.

Here is the chat transcript:

User
I have a problem and would need some coaching. Can you do that?

AI
I'd be happy to do that. My approach is to ask questions that can help you reflect on your current situation and find possible solutions. However, if you are looking for a coach who offers deeper emotional support or specialized techniques such as systemic or therapeutic coaching, a human coach might be more suitable.

How would you like to start? Are there specific topics you would like to discuss, or would you prefer to first describe your current situation?

User
Here is my problem: I have been working as an IT expert in a group of ten colleagues for three years. I enjoy the work and get along well with the others. My problem is that a month ago we got a new manager who only puts pressure on us and takes good per-

formance for granted. Although I continue to deliver good results, I receive no recognition for them. On the contrary, he repeatedly makes it clear to me that my current performance is not sufficient and must be improved. I am not the only one with this problem; the others are affected as well. Since I assume that I cannot change my manager, my only option is to look for another job, either within the company or elsewhere.

AI

This sounds like a challenging situation that understandably causes stress and dissatisfaction. If I understand your description correctly, on the one hand, you are burdened by the lack of respect and recognition from the new manager. On the other hand, there is the question of how you want to orient yourself in the long term: an internal transfer or a job change outside the company.

To support you further in the coaching process, we could jointly explore the following perspectives and questions:

7

1. **Clarification of values and needs:** What is most important to you in your professional role and work environment? Is it about recognition, development opportunities, stability, or a sense of team? Reflecting on your values can help you make a more informed decision between an internal or external move.
2. **Analysis of options for action:** Are there internal departments or other positions that might appeal to you and where a more positive leadership style prevails? A change of perspective within the company could reduce the strain while preserving the benefits of your current work environment.
3. **Dealing with the manager and communication:** Even if you believe that a change in his behavior is unlikely, we could discuss how you might communicate your achievements and desire for recognition in an appropriate and appreciative manner. A professional feedback conversation with him could at least help to clarify the situation.
4. **Stress management and self-care:** Since the situation is already causing sleep problems, it would be sensible to find strategies for stress reduction that you can implement immediately. This could be a first step to reduce the pressure while you work on a long-term solution.

If any of these points are particularly relevant to you, or if you are drawn to a different perspective, we can gladly explore that in more detail.

User

I believe stress management and self-care are particularly important for me at the moment.

AI

In this case, it may be helpful to start directly with strategies that noticeably ease your daily routine and create space for recovery. Here are a few approaches you could try:

1. **Daily structure for recovery breaks:** Consciously integrate small breaks into your workday that are specifically tailored to your needs. These could be short breathing exercises, walks in the fresh air, or targeted movement exercises.

These interruptions help to reduce strain in the short term and lower stress levels.

2. **Mental detachment:** Develop small routines to mentally draw a line at the end of the workday. A brief ritual such as jotting down "closing thoughts" for the day or visualizing an internal "end-of-work switch" can help clear your mind.
3. **Relaxation techniques and mindfulness:** Techniques such as progressive muscle relaxation, autogenic training, or short mindfulness exercises (e.g., focusing on your breath for five minutes) can have an immediate calming effect and relieve the nervous system. If you are already familiar with any of these methods, it would be ideal to build on that; otherwise, a brief introduction can already be helpful.
4. **Setting boundaries, also in your private life:** Especially if your partner or other close individuals are adding extra pressure, it is important to set clear boundaries. Gently clarify that you are working on a solution yourself and appreciate support, but currently need stability to go through this process at your own pace.
5. **Focus on positive activities after work:** Deliberately plan activities that bring you joy and distract your thoughts from work. This could be a hobby, exercise, time with friends, or a creative project. Purposefully engaging with enjoyable things helps you gain distance and build resilience.

I am happy to continue supporting you in implementing these strategies and adapting them to your needs.

If you compare this chat with the Alpina chat, you will notice that here, too, every utterance of the chatbot consists of two parts. First, the last statement of the coachee is paraphrased. However, instead of following this paraphrase with a question, there is a metacommunicatively formulated prompt to the coachee to decide, with reference to several options, what should be discussed next.

In contrast to the chat with Alpina, the second part here is more closely connected in content to the first. The reason for this appears to be that the process is not controlled by an AI-internal prompt script that must be strictly followed, but rather by the probabilistically driven activation of *problem-solving knowledge.* This takes into account the specifics of the current conversation situation and is therefore presented in the form of *problem-solving-oriented process design knowledge.*

In this way, ChatGPT succeeds in conducting the coaching dialogue so that the ultimate decisions about process control remain in the hands of the coachees. They must decide which of the process design options offered by ChatGPT they want to pursue.

At this point, we are once again confronted with the problem that we discussed in detail in Chapters 5 and 6, namely the problem that non-coaching-specific chatbots were not primarily developed for coaching and therefore cannot sufficiently meet certain requirements of professional coaching.

This shortcoming becomes apparent in the above chat in that it remains unclear how the four options for further process design offered are justified from a coaching conceptual perspective and why they are better than, for example, the process design proposal developed in Chapter 5 using an AI-external prompt script.

If you then look at the five solution options for stress management and self-care that are subsequently offered, it immediately becomes apparent—the often-criticized tendency of non-coaching-specific chatbots to offer as many solution suggestions as possible, calculated probabilistically from their encyclopedic knowledge, without first conducting an appropriate problem analysis.

This confirms the previously stated assumption that the use of AI-internal prompt scripts is a conceptual dead end, i.e., that there is no solution—or can be no solution—to the fit problem of the conversation management method controlled by AI-internal prompt scripts.

Before we therefore set out in Chapter 8 to look for a fundamentally different solution, we will first— for a very specific reason—take a look at a completely different AI agent.

7.2 Coaching-specific AI agents with discriminative AI and coaching-diagnostic animal images

While Alpina and the other AI agents mentioned above use the possibilities of *generative AI,* the coaching AI agent developed by Christiane Kranz and Friederike Redlbacher from Symbolon AG in collaboration with Prof. Dr. Benjamin Paaßen and Dr. Sylke Piéch from the German Research Center for Artificial Intelligence (DFKI) is characterized by the use of *discriminative AI.*

As will become clear below, this does not solve the fit problem in conversation management, but rather exacerbates it.

Nevertheless, it is worthwhile to engage with this approach (■ Fig. 7.2). This is because it demonstrates that, in addition to the possibility of coaching-specific AI-internal prompt scripts, there is another option for developing coaching-specific AI agents, namely the conceptual development and use of *coaching-diagnostic animal images.*

The approach presented in this section is therefore characterized overall by the following:

- it is aimed exclusively at coachees,
- it makes use solely of the capabilities of *discriminative AI,*
- and therefore, the knowledge base of the AI agent is not determined by an LLM, but instead contains specialized knowledge.
- This specialized knowledge guides the written communication with the coachees,
- using an AI-internal script that contains fixed statements, i.e., questions and information,
- and links these with colorful animal images.

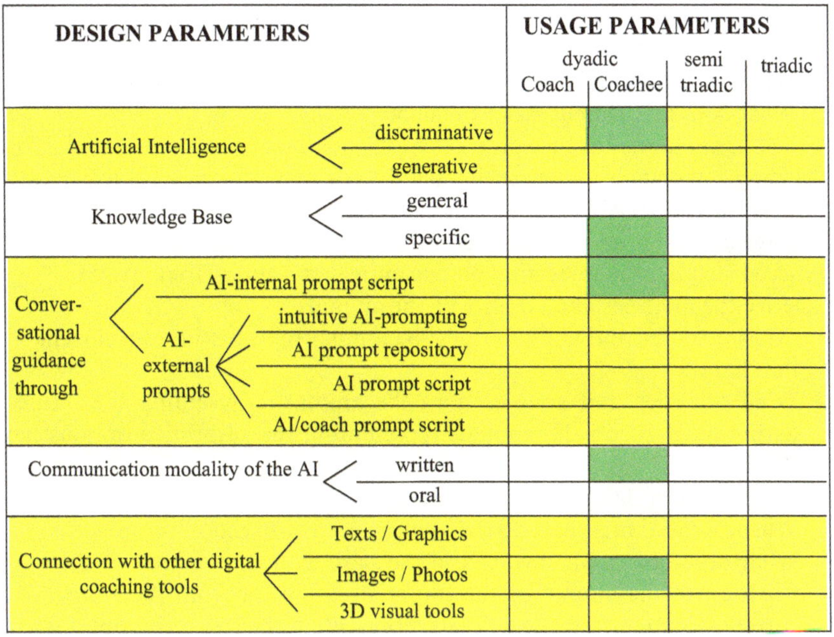

Fig. 7.2 Dyadic coaching AI agent with discriminatory AI and AI-internal prompt script

Based on discriminative AI, the information entered by the coachees is assigned to predefined categories, which in turn are linked to precisely defined output options of the AI agent. – The advantage of this is that hallucinations are excluded.

However, the associated weakness is that the conversation management tends to appear rather rigid, and the fit problem discussed in the previous section is further exacerbated.

This weakness is offset by the advantages of the coaching method used, i.e., the *Symbolon Method®* developed by Christiane Kranz. It builds on the psychology developed by Carl Gustav Jung and establishes a *double-loop coaching* approach that places the immersive contemplation of artworks or animal images at its methodological center by using them *for coaching diagnostics* (Kranz 2011a, b). In this way, coaching-diagnostic associations are stimulated, which encourage insights into the unconscious and direct attention to existential questions of meaning.

On this basis, the work with 14 available animal images is divided into the following six steps or tasks (Kranz 2011b):

- "In the first step, select an area, then a topic, and finally a question. The area is the context to which the topic and question relate. The topic can be a desire, a problem, or a pending decision." (Ibid., p. 28)
- Select from the available animal images the animal that corresponds to your current situation, as well as the one that visualizes your future situation (Ibid., p. 34)

- "Immerse yourself in your associations with the animal images."
  - "What does each animal trigger in me?
  - What are my thoughts, feelings, and associations with the animal?
  - What does this animal mean to me personally?"

  "All your spontaneous thoughts, feelings, and associations are essential for developing understanding. Even if they do not seem meaningful to you at first glance: Stay in touch with your mental connections and deepen them further by engaging even more intensively with each animal and your self-reflection. Proceed step by step, reflecting on one animal at a time. (Ibid., p. 35)
- "Derive the qualities and abilities of the animals."
  - What qualities and abilities does the animal representing the current situation have?
  - What qualities and abilities does the animal representing the future situation have, or do the animals representing the respective options have?" (Ibid., p. 36)

7

- "Recognize your development potential" (…)
  - What essential messages do the animals convey to me?
  - What development is involved in the path from the animal of the current situation to the animal of the future situation, or from the animal of the current situation to those animals representing the respective options?
  - Are there qualities of the animals that I reject in relation to my question? Do people involved in my question reject certain qualities of the animals? Are these qualities insufficiently present in the topic? If so, could these very qualities be helpful for further development or decision-making?
  - Which qualities and characteristics of the individual animals do I wish for myself and would like to integrate for myself or with regard to the topic?" (Ibid., p. 37)
- "Define your conclusions and solution steps. (…) What concrete possibilities for change, solutions, or decision-making bases do I see in relation to my topic and my question?" (Ibid., p. 38)

I tested this self-coaching approach as designed, and after registering, I received the following statement:

AI

Hi Harald, I am the AI-powered chatbot of Symbolon AG. Based on a script, I will guide you through your self-coaching process with coaching questions. You answer the questions step by step in the chat, or click by click.

During the coaching process, I do not generate any new, free-form texts. Instead, I select the next relevant question or statement from the wealth of quality-assured texts provided by Symbolon AG, based on your written responses. We are in a secure environment.

Allow all answers that come to mind spontaneously. What these answers trigger in you is just as relevant as what you think about them. Therefore, supplement your factual considerations with your imagination. Let your associations and feelings run free, even if what they trigger in you may seem nonsensical or strange at first glance. In the following steps, these impulses often lead to surprising and valuable insights. I cannot answer individual questions for you.

Take your time for your coaching and do not interrupt it. The coaching space is available to you for up to 2 hours at a time. Make sure you have a quiet environment and are not disturbed.

What makes this coaching special is that you are supported in the process by a work of art depicting 14 animals.

The coaching process consists of five steps:

1) You define your coaching topic and coaching goal.
2) You select and reflect on the animal that corresponds to your coaching topic.
3) You select and reflect on the animal that corresponds to your coaching goal.
4) You connect both animals and integrate the different aspects.
5) You summarize your insight.

At the end, you can download your result as a summary in PDF format once.

Now let's get started with the coaching topic.

To ensure the coaching delivers the greatest possible benefit for you, it is important that you first define your problem precisely in one sentence: What topic in your work situation do you want to develop a solution for? It must be a topic or problem that directly affects you. For example, 'I have a conflict with my supervisor' or 'I constantly feel stressed and under pressure'.

Please think carefully about what your professional topic or problem is and write it in one sentence in the chat. Start your sentence about the topic or problem with 'I ...'

Compared to the chats discussed in the previous section, it is noticeable that this initial communication contains a variety of different pieces of information and recommendations, and is therefore significantly more extensive.

As the following chat shows, this characteristic is typical for the Symbolon AI agent.

User

I have just completed a very comprehensive coaching training and now want to apply this knowledge and skill in working with coachees.

AI

Next, it is important that you think about your coaching goal and define it clearly: What do you want to achieve in the future with regard to your topic?

What should the future look like? This vision of the future must directly concern you and describe the state after the solution has been achieved. For example, 'I work constructively with my supervisor' or 'I am balanced and high-performing'.

Please think about your vision of the future and write it in one sentence in the chat. Start your sentence about the future vision with 'I ...'.

User
I want to have an average of 10 paying clients per month.

AI
Next, we move on to the animals. Put yourself in your initial situation and work attitude and look at the following picture with the animals. Think about your coaching topic that you have just defined: 'I have just completed a very comprehensive coaching training and now want to apply this knowledge and skill in working with coachees.'

Now choose the animal that best fits you and your feelings, regardless of whether you know the animal well. It is not about judgments such as right or wrong, better or worse. It is about your perception and the feelings triggered by the animal. Your choice is essential for the following coaching process.

Look at the individual animals, tune in to yourself, and choose the animal that best fits your coaching topic and your current situation, 'I have just completed a very comprehensive coaching training and now want to apply this knowledge and skill in working with coachees.' Click on the animal you choose.

User
Lion

AI
Thank you. Now we will start reflecting on the lion, which represents your current situation. Take your time to get to know the lion and gain insights. Imagine yourself as the lion. Perceive your thoughts, associations, and feelings as the lion and answer the following questions in the chat:

What are you, Harald, particularly good at as the lion in your imagination?

User
I am good at spotting potential prey and am very strong in close combat, i.e., in direct contact with other people.

AI
What do you find difficult as the lion?

User
I have trouble getting close enough to the prey.

AI
Let the first two answers sink in. How do these strengths and difficulties show up in yourself and in your professional life?

User
I am creative and assertive in direct contact with others. But I have a marketing problem: getting close enough to my target group.

AI

That is understandable.

Continue to imagine that you, Harald, are the lion. What do you need as the lion to feel comfortable?

User

Enough food for myself and my young.

AI

What do your last answers trigger when you transfer them to your current situation, 'I have just completed a very comprehensive coaching training and now want to apply this knowledge and skill in working with coachees'?

User

Frustration and lack of direction.

AI

Now let's move on to the characteristics and special features of the lion: The lion belongs to the family of cats and predators. It claims the highest rank in its pride and defends its territory against intruders. The lionesses take care of the offspring and hunt together. The lion is the first to feed on the prey. A lion can weigh up to 250 kg and has no natural enemies.

Next, we will list the symbolic aspects and principles that the lion represents. …

Even though the above chat transcript only refers to the beginning of the entire coaching dialogue, it is already clearly apparent that the *fit problem* in the Alpina chat described in the previous section is even more pronounced. This becomes particularly evident at the end of the above chat transcript, when the AI agent does not respond to the coachee's emotions, but instead, without any transition, proceeds to the next work step and presents general characteristics of lions.

On the other hand, the Symbolon Method® and the corresponding AI-internal prompt script are characterized by the fact that animal images are meaningfully used for the *coaching-diagnostic analysis* of the current actual situation and the target situation desired by the coachees, and that the principles of *double-loop coaching* are conceptually applied as a foundation.

References

Kranz C (2011a) Durch Selbstreflexion zum Erfolg, 2. Aufl. Symbolon, Wien

Kranz C (2011b) Tierisches Potenzial. Selbstreflexion mit Tierbildern. Symbolon Verlag, Wien

Malafronte O (2024) PocketConfidant AI. In: Passmore J, Diller SJ, Isaacson S, Brantl M (Hrsg) The Digital and AI Coaches' handbook. Routledge, London/New York, S 345–348

Mai V, Rutschmann R (2023a) Chatbots im Coaching. Potenziale und Einsatzmöglichkeiten von digitalen Coaching-Begleitern und Assistenten. Z Organisationsentwickl, Superv, Coach 30:45–57. ▸ https://link.springer.com/article/10.1007/s11613-022-00801-3

Mai V, Rutschmann R (2023b) Best Practices im Chatbot Coaching. Einblicke in Forschung und Entwicklung des StudiCoachBots der TH Köln und in die Coaching Chatbot Plattform evoach. Z Organisationsentwickl, Superv, Coach 30:111–125. ▶ https://doi.org/10.1007/s11613-022-00802-2

Novic H (2024) Rocky AI. In: Passmore J, Diller SJ, Isaacson S, Brantl M (Hrsg) The Digital and AI Coaches' handbook. Routledge, London/New York, S 349–352

Rutschmann R (2024) AI coaching: the next generation (Part2). ▶ https://www.linkedin.com/pulse/ai-coaching-next-generation-part2-rebecca-rutschmann-pqgje/. Zugegriffen am 16.10.2024

Terblanche N (2020) A design framework to create artificial intelligence coaches'. Inter J Evid Based Coaching Ment 18(2):152–165. ▶ https://doi.org/10.24384/b7gs-3h05

Terblanche N (2024a) Artificial intelligence coaching chatbots. In: Passmore J, Diller SJ, Isaacson S, Brantl M (Hrsg) The Digital and AI Coaches' handbook. Routledge, London/New York, S 101–109

Terblanche N (2024b) Artificial Intelligence (AI) Coaching: redefining people development and organizational performance. J Appl Behav Sci:1–8. ▶ https://doi.org/10.1177/00218863241283919

Triadic AI Coaching with Coaching Diagnostic Knowledge and External AI Prompt Script

Contents

H. Geissler, *AI-Coaching*,
https://doi.org/10.1007/978-3-658-49178-9_8

In the last three chapters, it was shown and discussed,
- how non-coaching-specific chatbots can be successfully used with the help of coaching-specific, AI-external prompts or prompt scripts,
- but at the same time, how one is confronted with the problems of encyclopedic general knowledge of non-coaching-specific chatbots,
- how this issue can be overcome with the help of AI-internal prompt scripts,
- but in doing so, the problem of fit must be accepted, i.e., the problem that the coaching processes generated in this way often do not fit well with the specific coaching issue at hand,
- and that it is beneficial to equip AI agents with coaching diagnostic capabilities.

On this basis, the following section presents an approach that incorporates and further develops these insights, namely *triadic AI coaching with coaching diagnostic knowledge and an AI-external prompt script that links coach prompts with AI prompts.*

At the center of this approach is an AI agent that functions as a coach assistant and is therefore referred to as the *"Artificial Intelligence Coach Assistant (AI-CA)"*.

8

As shown in Fig. 8.1, this approach differs from those previously discussed in that,
- *three parties* are involved here, namely coaches, coachees, and an AI agent, which coaches and coachees systematically integrate into their dialogue,
- this AI agent is based on *generative AI,*
- and not only has access to the *general knowledge* of ChatGPT,
- but also possesses *coaching-specific knowledge.* In contrast to the AI agents introduced in ▶ Ch. 7, this is not knowledge or skills for coaching-methodological process design, but rather *coaching diagnostic* knowledge.
- Users, i.e., coaches and coachees, can activate this knowledge using *intuitive AI prompts*
- and are additionally—and crucially—supported by an *AI-external prompt script* that links tasks for the coaches with tasks they assign to the AI agent.
- In this way, it is also possible to integrate other digital coaching tools.

With this design and usage profile, triadic AI coaching builds on the advantages of the approaches presented so far while avoiding their disadvantages (Geißler 2024; Terblanche 2024), not least through a productive division of labor between the coach and the AI agent. By relieving the coach of the responsibility for creating resource-intensive structures—such as criteria-based summaries or personalized experience reports—and for providing coaching diagnostic insights and suitable problem-solving suggestions, the AI agent gives the coach more freedom and resources for higher-level process management and for maintaining an intensive *working relationship* with the coachees.

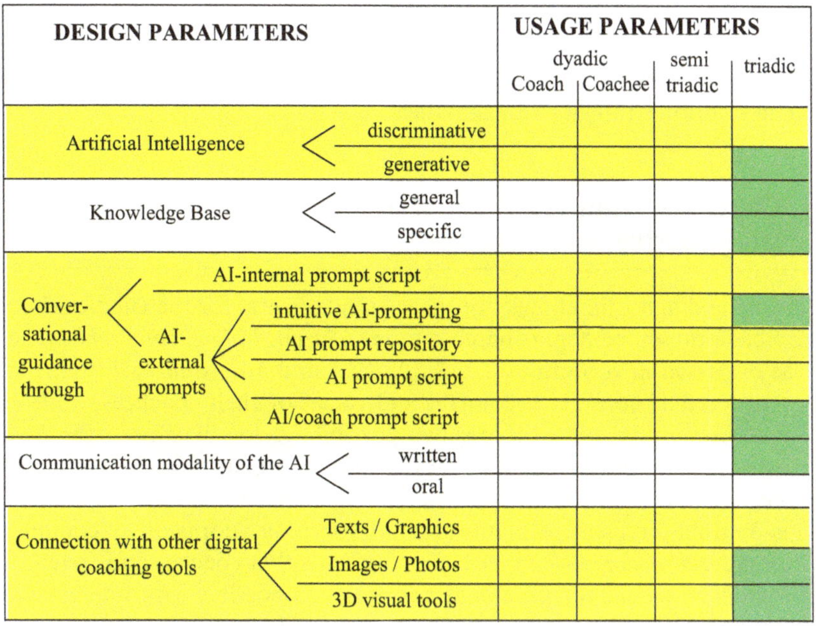

Fig. 8.1 Triadic AI coaching with coaching diagnostic knowledge and an AI-external prompt script that links coach prompts with AI prompts

8.1 Coaching Diagnostic Knowledge

In ▶ Sect. 2.2.1 it was explained that generative AI is based on mathematical models, i.e., large language models (LLMs), which represent reality using artificial neural networks with numerous trainable parameters. These parameters are adjusted to the input training data during the training process of program development, enabling LLMs to recognize complex patterns and structures in the data and to generate corresponding output based on this foundation.

This training can consist of two consecutive phases, in which first *encyclopedic world knowledge* is imparted and then specialized knowledge, such as coaching-*specific knowledge,* is added.

As shown in the previous chapter, this may involve *coaching-methodological process design knowledge,* i.e., knowledge about how to methodically structure the dialogue with coachees based on a particular coaching theory. As has become clear above, the major weakness of this knowledge is that it must refer to coaching theories that include recommendations or instructions on how the coaching process can be methodically standardized.

Not least, the practical trials in the previous chapter have shown that such standardization is problematic, because the chosen methodological approach often does not fit the specific characteristics of the coaching issue at hand and the current state of the coachees.

For this reason, another type of coaching-specific knowledge is necessary, namely *coaching diagnostic knowledge,* i.e., knowledge about the possible causes underlying the present coaching issues, as well as knowledge about the corresponding solution strategies and activities.

8.1.1 Coaching Diagnostics as Dialectical Situational Diagnostics

The coaching diagnostic knowledge that is fundamental for the triadic AI coaching approach presented here is based on the *Coaching Alignment Problem,* i.e., on the – as discussed in ▶ Sections 2.1, 2.2.1, 2.2.2 and 3.1 – dual task that coaches must appropriately consider the norms and values of their coachees, while at the same time keeping in mind the positive possibilities for their personal development, especially those possibilities that the coachees themselves do not spontaneously see.

8 This dual requirement, which triadic AI coaching adopts as its commitment to the paradigm of *double-loop coaching,* demands that coaches and coachees develop a *problem-solving orientation* as concretely as possible with reference to the *situations* in which the coachees' problems primarily arise. This must relate, on the one hand, to root cause analysis and, on the other, to the subsequent development of an appropriate solution strategy and implementation support.

The knowledge that coachees need, and that they must develop with the help of their coaches or with the support of the AI agent working with the coach, is therefore *situationally diagnostic, problem-solving-oriented knowledge.*

At the center of this coaching situational diagnostics are two interrelated tasks. The first consists in capturing, with regard to the specifics of the situations perceived as problematic, the full range of possible orientations available.

The second task is to recognize the norms and values of the various possible orientations and their underlying polarity, and to make a decision based on these that is characterized by a good balance of the polar-opposite norms and values.

This idea connects to the concept of the so-called *Values and Development Square,* which Schulz von Thun (1989) adopted from Paul Helwig (1967) and his *dialectical thinking.* The premise of this concept, which ultimately goes back to Aristotelian dialectics, is the insight that

> "(...) every value (every virtue, every guiding principle, every personality trait) can only have a constructive effect if it exists in a state of *sustained tension* with a positive counter-value, a 'sister virtue'. Instead of sustained tension, one can also speak of *balance.* Without this sustained tension (balance), a value degenerates into its 'degenerated form' (Helwig) – or, to put it differently: into its *devalued exaggeration.*" (Schulz von Thun 1989, p. 38)

Schulz von Thun illustrates this basic idea using the example of *stinginess,* showing that stinginess is a *normative problem-solving orientation* that is not well balanced with its normative or value-based opposite, *prodigality.* In order to achieve a good balance, it is therefore necessary to reconstruct and develop the previously unexpressed positive cores of these two extremes, namely, on the one hand, *thrift* and, on the other hand, *generosity* (ibid., p. 39).

This problem-solving strategy is based on the assumption that personal and social developments always take place within a *dialectical field of tension* between different alternatives. It is therefore wise, especially with regard to one's own personal development, to ask about the normative or value-based orientation of every decision to be made in a given situation, and to productively relate it to its respective normative opposite.

In order to make practical use of this insight in coaching, a clear *situational typology* is necessary, which makes it possible to adequately capture the infinite variety of different situations.

One way to develop this is to refer to the *existential fundamental and life questions* that confront all people across cultures and times, and to identify the respective normative or value-based poles of orientation that need to be balanced.

In this sense, 23 fundamental and life questions have been reconstructed, such as:

- In which situations should one, to what extent, in what way, and why, be fully present in the here and now with all senses, or focus entirely on the positive possibilities of the future?
- In which situations should one, to what extent, in what way, and why, make decisions rationally or intuitively?
- In which situations should one, to what extent, in what way, and why, orient one's behavior toward preservation or change?
- In which situations should one evaluate oneself critically or positively, to what extent, in what way, and why?

As the above examples show, each of these existential fundamental and life questions contains a normative or value-based polarity that must be balanced with regard to the specifics of the respective situation. In this way, the 23 reconstructed fundamental and life questions sensitize us to 46 possible core problems, which always arise when the necessary balance is not achieved and one polarity dominates excessively at the expense of its opposite.

On this conceptual basis, the use of the situational diagnostic knowledge underlying triadic AI coaching can unfold in the following steps:

- Clarification of which of the 23 possible existential fundamental and life questions primarily underlie the present coaching issue;
- Clarification of which normative or value-based orientations the situationally prevailing problem-solving activities are excessively aligned with;
- Reconstruction of the neglected or suppressed normative or value-based opposites;
- Reconstruction of the positive cores of the normative or value-based orientations that excessively dominate the situationally prevailing problem-solving activities;

- Clarification of how these positive cores can be connected, i.e., reconciled, in a problem-solving way with the situationally neglected or suppressed normative or value-based opposites.

8.1.2 Example: How critically or positively should one evaluate oneself in certain situations?

The following section aims to illustrate the thoughts presented above using the example of the dialectic involved in dealing with the question of in which situations, to what extent, and in what manner one should evaluate oneself critically or positively—and why.

As illustrated in Fig. 8.2 below, it is useful to represent the concept of the Values and Development Square developed by Schulz von Thun as a trapezoid, whose upper line symbolizes the maximum degree of *problem-generating tensions* that arise from an overly one-sided balancing.

With regard to the existential fundamental and life question chosen here as an example, this means that two core problems can arise from a situationally overly one-sided balancing, namely

- the core problem of an *inferiority complex,* i.e., in certain situations, inappropriately assuming one's own inferiority and therefore, without reality-checking, a priori and categorically assessing one's own achievements, abilities, and potential as inferior,

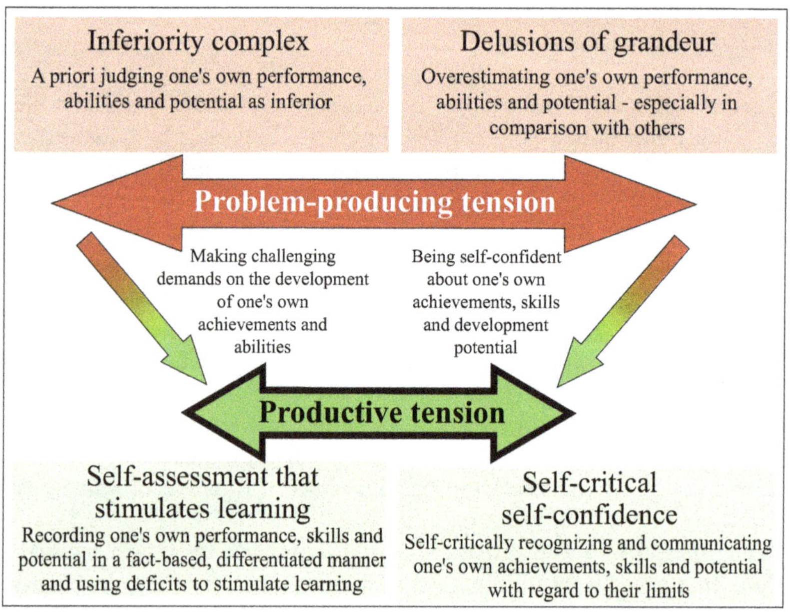

Fig. 8.2 The dialectic of dealing with the question of how critically or positively one should evaluate oneself

- and the opposite core problem of *megalomania,* i.e., in certain situations, inappropriately assuming one's own greatness and therefore unrealistically overestimating one's own achievements, abilities, and potential—especially in comparison with others.

The next important piece of information documented in the trapezoid of ◘ Fig. 8.2 is the *positive core,*

- which, on the one hand, is latently present in the problem-generating extreme positions but is still completely underdeveloped,
- and, on the other hand, is excessively developed and therefore becomes a problem.

With regard to the fundamental and life question discussed here, this makes it clear that

- in the (in certain situations adopted) extreme position of assuming one's own inferiority, the positive core—excessively and one-sidedly developed—lies in setting challenging demands for the development of one's own achievements and abilities
- and that—conversely—in the (in certain situations adopted) opposite extreme position of assuming one's own greatness, the positive core lies in confidently standing by one's own achievements, competencies, and development potential.

To overcome such situation-specific balancing problems, it is necessary to *reconcile the previously opposing normative antipodes* in order to *transform the problem-reproducing tension into a productive tension.*

For the extreme position of the inferiority complex, this means

- bringing one's own positive core—which in certain situations is excessively and one-sidedly developed—into a productive tension with the positive core of the normative antipode
- and, in this way, considering the *solution strategy of learning-stimulating self-evaluation,* i.e., to record one's own achievements, abilities, and potential in a fact-based and differentiated manner and to use deficits as learning stimuli.

For the opposite extreme position of megalomania, on the other hand, this means

- bringing one's own positive core—which is also excessively and one-sidedly developed in certain situations—into a productive tension with the positive core of the normative antipode
- and, in this way, considering the *solution strategy of self-critical self-confidence,* i.e., to recognize and communicate one's own achievements, abilities, and potential self-critically with regard to their limitations.

With regard to this basic structure, which is identical in the development of all existential fundamental and life questions, *text modules* can be written, with the help of which the AI agent of triadic coaching, i.e., the "Artificial Intelligence Coach Assistant (AI-CA)",

- can organize the input data of the problem description in terms of content,
- can conduct corresponding problem analyses
- and, on this basis, can identify problem-solving activities.

In detail, it is important that a separate text module is written for each fundamental or life question, that all text modules have the same basic structure, and that they are cross-referenced in terms of content. Only in this way can the AI agent optimally utilize the coaching-diagnostic knowledge provided.

8.2 The AI-External Prompt Script

8

In addition to the coaching-diagnostic knowledge, triadic AI coaching is characterized by a second fundamental conceptual feature, namely an *AI-external prompt script* (Fig. 8.3). This consists of ten multi-part tasks (prompts-clusters) that relate to the four phases of the coaching process, i.e.,
- problem and goal description,
- problem analysis and the development of outlines for the solution strategy,
- the concretization of this solution strategy
- and finally, support in the practical implementation of the chosen solution strategy and solution activities.

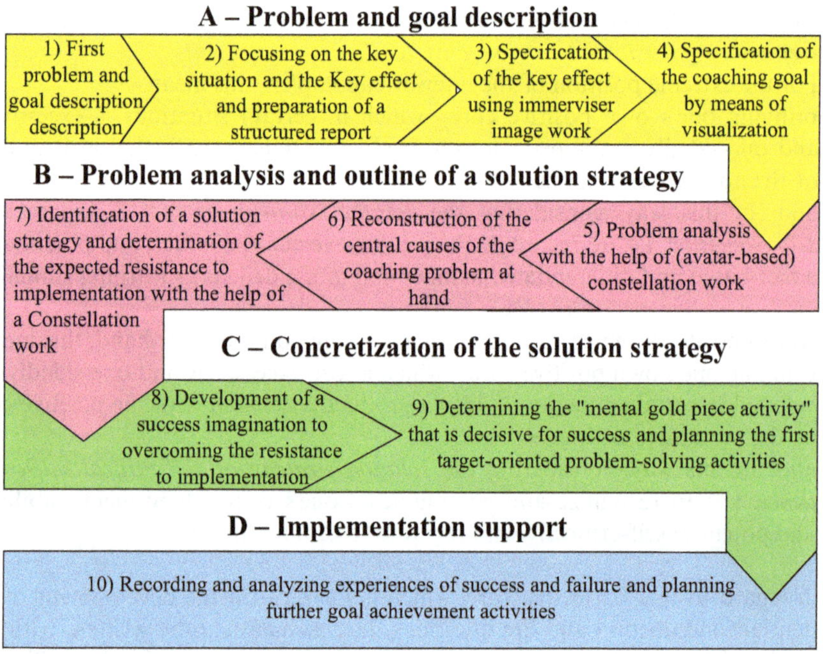

Fig. 8.3 The AI-external prompt script of triadic AI coaching

As already explained in ▶ Section 6.1, each of these ten prompt-clusters initially includes a coach prompt, in which the coach is instructed to behave in a specific coaching-methodological manner during the interaction with the coachees.

This interaction results in the creation of a protocol, which the coach sends to the AI agent together with a specific pre-formulated processing request. This is the AI prompt, which instructs the AI to produce a specific output based on the submitted protocol, using its general and coaching-diagnostic knowledge.

The subsequent step is again guided by a coach prompt. In this step, the coach and coachee provide feedback to the AI agent by discussing the output received and modifying it so that it exactly reflects the coachee's perspective. In line with the *"human-in-the-loop" approach,* the AI agent can thus learn to tailor itself to the conditions and perspectives of the coachees.

The first of these ten mega-prompts is as follows:

Task 1: Initial Assessment of the Target-Actual Situation

Coach Prompt: <Coach greets coachee, engages in some small talk, and then shares the screen to empathetically introduce the concept and process of AI coaching in a manner appropriate for the coachee. The coach pays particular attention to building a positive working relationship. In this context, the coach gives the coachee sufficient space to determine how much "technologically undisturbed" space the coachee needs to present their issue—or how helpful it might be to simultaneously document the presentation of the issue.>

Coach Prompt: <Coach encourages coachee to describe the currently unsatisfactory ACTUAL situation and how they envision the TARGET situation. The coach limits themselves to active listening.>

AI Prompt: I have the following problem or coaching goal: …

[Coach summarizes the coachee's description of the actual and target situation in writing and sends it to ChatGPT.]

AI Prompt: Can you help me?

Specifically, this prompt-cluster consists of several individual prompts, each aligned with different profiles targeting the success factors presented in ▶ Section 6.1:

- The first angle bracket contains an initial coach prompt, which, in addition to the success factor of emotional support, primarily focuses on the success factor of process management.
- The second coach prompt, formulated in the second angle bracket, focuses on a specific combination of the three success factors: goal clarification, problem and self-reflection, and emotional support.
- This is followed by the instruction for protocol creation, which is somewhat more narrowly focused on the success factors of goal clarification and problem and self-reflection. The instruction is that the protocol must begin with the words: "I have the following problem or coaching goal." The coach must copy these words into the AI, together with the following square bracket.

The text within the bracket, which describes the content focus of the protocol, is overwritten by the coach, who enters the relevant content in the square bracket.
- This is followed by the AI prompt: "Can you help me?"

Following this, the second prompt-cluster serves to deepen the assessment and structuring of the target-actual situation of the coaching issue and is accordingly divided into several coach and AI prompts.

8

Task 2: In-Depth Assessment and Structuring of the Target-Actual Situation

Coach Prompt: <Coach gives coachee space to reflect on the response from the coaching AI, asks what the response evokes internally, and documents the key statements.>

AI Prompt: Thank you for your comments. They have spontaneously triggered the following in me: ...

[Coach documents, in the presence of the coachee, how the coachee responded emotionally and cognitively to the comments.]

Coach Prompt: <Coach stops screen sharing and encourages coachee to focus cognitively and emotionally on the "key situations" in which the problem occurs particularly intensely or frequently, and then explores the "key affect," i.e., the intrapsychic processes the coachee perceives in these "key situations.">

AI Prompt: Here is some additional information about my issue: ...

[Coach documents the coachee's description of the "key situations" and the "key affect," discusses the protocol with the coachee, and shares it with the coaching AI.]

AI Prompt: Please create a report written in the first person, summarizing all information to date regarding the problem and goal description. Structure this report in two parts, first describing the current ACTUAL situation and then the TARGET situation I desire. In each part, refer—where possible—to the following aspects:
- the existing external conditions and external resources, including my physical conditions,
- my psychological processes (such as feelings, motivational impulses, and thoughts) that are currently triggered in me by the coaching issue,
- my observable behaviors that are currently triggered in me by the coaching issue,
- and the actual consequences that my observable behaviors cause for those around me and for myself.

Coach Prompt: <Coach gives coachee space to reflect on the response from the coaching AI, asks what the response evokes internally, and documents the key statements.>

AI Prompt: Thank you for your comments. They have spontaneously triggered the following in me: ...

[Coach documents, in the presence of the coachee, how the coachee responded emotionally and cognitively to the comments.]

AI Prompt: I am adopting your "structured report of the ACTUAL and TARGET situation" with the following modifications: ...
[Coach copies the AI's response from Task 2 and documents the changes requested by the coachee.]

Task 3: In-Depth Exploration of the "Key Affect" Using Immersive Image Work

Coach Prompt: <Coach explains the next steps to the coachee and, using screen sharing, shows several images or photos, asking the coachee to select the one that is best suited to visualize the present "key affect.">
Coach Prompt: <Coach conducts an immersive image viewing session with the coachee.>
AI Prompt: I have selected a suitable image for my "key affect," which I describe as follows: ...
[I chose the image because xxx. I see xxxx in the image. When I immerse myself in the image, then xxxxx. My attention is especially drawn to xxxxx and I hear within myself the words: "xxxxx."]
AI Prompt: My task for you is as follows: once again summarize the "key affect" described above, establish an internal connection between this "key affect" and the image description just provided, and refine the description of the "key affect" on this basis.

Task 4: In-depth Exploration of the Coaching Goal Using Immersive Image Work

Coach Prompt: <Coach gives the coachee space to reflect on the response from the coaching AI, asks what the response evokes internally, and records the key statements.>
AI Prompt: Thank you for your explanations. They have spontaneously triggered the following in me: ...
[Coach records, in the presence of the coachee, how the coachee responded emotionally and cognitively to the explanations.]
AI Prompt: I am adopting your refined description of the "key affect" with the following modifications: ...
[Coach copies the AI response from Task 3 and makes the changes requested by the coachee.]
Coach Prompt: <Coach offers the coachee several images or photos to visualize their goal and then conducts an immersive viewing of the selected image or photo with the coachee.>
AI Prompt: I have also selected a suitable image for my coaching goal, which I describe as follows: ...
[I chose the image because xxx. In the image, I see xxx. When I immerse myself experientially in the image, then xxx. My focus is especially on xxx and I hear within myself the words: "xxxxx".]

AI Prompt: First, tell me how the description of this image relates to the description of my coaching goal, and second, make a suggestion for a correspondingly refined description of my coaching goal.
Coach Prompt: <Coach gives the coachee space to reflect on the response from the coaching AI, asks what the response evokes internally, and records the key statements.>
AI Prompt: Thank you for your explanations. They have spontaneously triggered the following in me: ...
[Coach records, in the presence of the coachee, how the coachee responded emotionally and cognitively to the explanations.]
AI Prompt: I am adopting your refined description with the following modifications: ...
[Coach copies the AI response from Task 4 and makes the changes requested by the coachee.]

Task 5: Reconstruction of the "Vicious Cycle" Using Constellation Work

Coach Prompt: <Coach explains to the coachee the concept of the "Inner Team" and the psychodramatic in-depth interview, which is then conducted with the coachee.>
Coach Prompt: <Coach conducts the psychodramatic in-depth interview with the coachee.>
AI Prompt: I conducted an in-depth interview with my coach, based on the Inner Team model. The goal of the interview is to clarify, with regard to the "key situation," which of my personality parts support my coaching goal and which cause the "key affect" that hinders or prevents the pursuit and achievement of this goal.
[Coach inserts the transcript of the interview into GPT.]
Coach Prompt: <Coach explains the concept of the "vicious cycle" to the coachee.>
Coach Prompt: <Coach encourages the coachee to identify their own "vicious cycle" and limits themselves to active listening.>
AI Prompt: Assume that the tensions between the two personality parts, which become apparent in the transcribed in-depth interview, illuminate the core area of the present coaching issue.
Using the "vicious cycle" text module, reconstruct the problem-stabilizing "vicious cycle" of the present coaching issue. Refer both to the transcribed interview and to all individual pieces of information regarding the present coaching issue.

Task 6: Reconstruction of the Central Balancing Problems

Coach Prompt: <Coach gives the coachee space to reflect on the response from the coaching AI, asks what the response evokes internally, and records the key statements.>

AI Prompt: Thank you for your explanations. They have spontaneously triggered the following in me:
[Coach records, in the presence of the coachee, how the coachee responded emotionally and cognitively to the explanations.]
Coach Prompt: <If necessary, the following follow-up questions are asked to ChatGPT:
What exactly do you mean by xxx?
Or:
Please state the information from my coaching issue on which you base your assessment that xxx?>
AI Prompt: Thank you for your answers. On this basis, I am adopting your analysis with the following modifications: …
[Coach copies the AI response from Task 5 and makes the changes requested by the coachee.]
AI Prompt: Please analyze, using the "balancing problems" text module as well as the other uploaded text modules, which balancing problems are central to my coaching issue.

Task 8: Development of a Success Imagination

Coach Prompt: <Coach gives the coachee space to reflect on the response from the coaching AI, asks what the response evokes internally, and records the key statements.>
AI Prompt: Thank you for your explanations. They have spontaneously triggered the following in me: …
[Coach records, in the presence of the coachee, how the coachee responded emotionally and cognitively to the explanations.]
AI Prompt: Please describe, in one—and really only one—sentence as precisely as possible the "mental gold nugget activity" that will enable me to practically achieve the targeted strengthening of certain complementary forces.
Describe the consequences of this positive change in a personal experiential narrative written in the first person. I want to use this as a success imagination from now on.
In this success imagination, describe everything in a very detailed, vivid, and personal way, so that it can be imagined as concretely as in a film—everything that is outwardly observable and everything that happens intrapsychically within me. The experiential narrative starts with the "key situation," which has not changed. So, base the description on the "key situation" I shared with you at the beginning of this chat. In your description of the success imagination, also refer to the two images I chose for my current and desired situations.
In this sense, create two clearly distinct experiential descriptions as suggestions for two clearly different success imaginations.

Task 9: Identification of the Next Target-Oriented Activities

Coach Prompt: <Coach gives the coachee space to reflect on the response from the coaching AI, asks how the answer affects them internally, and records the key statements.>

AI Prompt: Thank you for your explanations. They have spontaneously triggered the following in me: …

[Coach records, in the presence of the coachee, how the coachee has responded emotionally and cognitively to the explanations.]

I prefer the following success visualization with the following modifications and will use it for my mental training in the coming days: …

[Coach copies the selected version and makes the changes requested by the coachee.]

AI Prompt: I will adopt your formulation of the "Gold Nugget Activity" with the following modifications: …

[Coach copies the AI's formulation of the Gold Nugget Activity and makes the changes requested by the coachee.]

8

AI Prompt: In the coming days, I want to try to carry out problem-solving actions that will enable me to achieve my coaching goal as quickly and sustainably as possible. The focus of these problem-solving actions must be the recently identified mental "Gold Nugget Activity."

Therefore, I am assigning you the task of offering me three – but really only three, no more – meaningful problem-solving actions in this sense. They must be as concrete as possible and closely linked to the information available regarding my current coaching issue.

Coach Prompt: <Coach gives the coachee space to reflect on the response from the coaching AI, asks how the answer affects them internally, and records the key statements.>

AI Prompt: Based on your suggestions, I am planning the following problem-solving activities for the coming days: …

[Coach records the coachee's problem-solving activities.

Additionally, the coach records how this planning affects the coachee internally.]

AI Prompt: Please save this without any comment. I will get back to you in the next few days and report on how well the implementation went.

Task 10: Implementation Support

Coach Prompt: <Coach asks the coachee about their experiences implementing the planned problem-solving activities, initially focusing on successes.>

AI Prompt: In implementing my planned problem-solving activities, I had the following success experience: …

[Coach records the most important success experience and clarifies how and to what extent it was causally influenced by the "Gold Nugget Activity" of the success visualization, and what percentage of the coaching goal and learning and development goal the coachee has currently achieved.]

Coach Prompt: <Coach asks the coachee about their experiences implementing the planned problem-solving activities, initially focusing on failures.>
AI Prompt: In implementing my planned problem-solving activities, I had the following failure experience: …
[Coach records the coachee's most important failure experience.]
AI Prompt: Tell me what I can learn, with regard to the "mental Gold Nugget Activity" of my success visualization and – where applicable – with regard to my previous successes, in order to be more successful in similar situations in the future. Please also use the text modules "Success Factors" and "Complementary Forces."
Coach Prompt: <Coach gives the coachee space to reflect on the response from the coaching AI, asks how the answer affects them internally, and records the key statements
AI Prompt: Thank you for your explanations. They have spontaneously triggered the following in me:
[Coach records, in the presence of the coachee, how the coachee has responded emotionally and cognitively to the explanations.]
AI Prompt: I agree with your analysis and the consequences you have suggested, with the following modifications: …
[Coach copies the AI's response and makes the changes requested by the coachee.]
AI Prompt: Please save this without any comment. I will get back to you in the next few days and let you know how things have progressed.

8.3 Practical Example

The prompt script presented in the previous section can lead to coach-coachee dialogues that include, for example, the following chat sequences:

- Task 1: Initial Assessment of the Target-Actual Situation

User

I have the following problem:
(I have been working as an IT specialist in a group with ten colleagues for three years. I enjoy the work and get along well with the others. My problem is that a month ago we got a new boss who only puts pressure on us and takes good performance for granted. Even though I continue to deliver good results, I receive no recognition for it. On the contrary, he repeatedly makes it clear that my current performance is not sufficient and must be improved. I am not the only one with this problem; the others feel the same way. Since I assume that I cannot change my boss, my only option is to look for another job, either within the company or elsewhere.)
Can you help me?

AI

Thank you for entrusting me with your concern. Your situation is undoubtedly stressful, but not uncommon. It touches on some fundamental questions that many people face: How do you deal with unfulfilled needs for recognition? And how can you continue to develop in an environment that offers little appreciation, without losing yourself in the process? These are existential questions that may be occupying you.

If I understand your description correctly, you enjoy your work and have good relationships with your colleagues. But for the past month, you have been dealing with a new boss who exerts pressure and does not acknowledge your performance. Although you continue to do good work, you are not experiencing the appreciation you desire. You are considering whether changing jobs – within or outside the company – is the only solution, since you assume you cannot change your boss.

Although I would need some additional information about your current issue in order to assess it appropriately and develop a solution, I already have the impression that you are currently doing a lot of things right and that you possess certain positive abilities that others might even envy. By this I mean that you are able to continue delivering good performance and maintain your motivation despite the pressure. This demonstrates a high level of intrinsic motivation and self-management skills.

8

The core problem may be that, so far, it has not been sufficiently possible to relate this ability of self-management to other important problem-solving criteria, such as dealing with external pressure and balancing self-expectations with external demands. It seems that the pursuit of external recognition may be in conflict with your internal self-management.

I would be happy to help you, together with your coach, to improve this balance so that you can find a solution that feels right for you.

- Task 2: In-Depth Assessment and Structuring of the Target-Actual Situation

User

Thank you very much for your explanations. They have spontaneously triggered the following in me:

[I feel well understood with this initial analysis, and it does me good to hear something positive about myself.]

Here are a few more details:

[I particularly struggle with my issue when I have put a lot of effort into my tasks, but at the same time am not entirely sure if I have done everything completely correctly. In these moments, I need some kind of guidance from my manager. In these situations, which I will refer to as "key situations" below, I always react very nervously and can only use my intellectual abilities to a limited extent. This "key effect" annoys me immensely and makes me even more insecure.]

Create a report written in the first person that summarizes all information available so far regarding the problem and goal description. Structure this report in two parts by first describing the current AS-IS situation and then the desired TO-BE situation. In each of the two parts, refer—as far as possible—to the following aspects:

- *to the existing external conditions and external resources, including my physical conditions,*
- *to my psychological processes (such as feelings, motivational impulses, and thoughts) that are currently triggered in me by the present coaching issue,*

- *to my observable behaviors that are currently triggered in me by the present coaching issue,*
- *and to the actual consequences that my observable behaviors cause for those around me and for myself.*

AI

Part 1: AS-IS Situation

External Conditions and Resources

I have been working as an IT specialist in a team of ten colleagues for three years. I generally enjoy my work and have a good relationship with my team. A month ago, our team got a new manager who exerts a lot of pressure through his leadership style. He takes good performance for granted and gives little to no recognition, even for positive results. Even though I continue to carry out my tasks carefully and with commitment, I feel that my efforts are not appreciated. What is particularly stressful is that I become insecure in certain situations when I am not sure whether my work meets my manager's expectations.

Psychological Processes

My main problem arises in key situations where I am working on complex tasks and am not sure if I have done everything correctly. In these moments, I feel very nervous and tense. Although I do my work to the best of my ability, the uncertainty about the expected results puts me under enormous pressure. In these key situations, I experience a kind of "key effect": my nervousness prevents me from fully utilizing my intellectual abilities, which further increases my frustration and insecurity. The feeling of being dependent on my manager's feedback makes me even more tense, because this feedback often does not come or is negative.

Observable Behaviors

When I am in one of these key situations, I often react nervously and reservedly. My behavior is strongly influenced by the uncertainty of whether my work meets expectations. This uncertainty is evident in my less confident demeanor and my inner stress, which is also visible externally. Sometimes I withdraw when I feel I am not getting clear guidance. In conversations with my manager, I seek affirmation, which rarely comes.

Actual Consequences

The effects of my behavior are twofold: On the one hand, I feel increasingly insecure and frustrated, which impacts my performance and motivation. Although I continue to do good work, my ability to realize my full potential is limited in key situations. This leads to additional stress, as I live with the feeling that I am not sufficiently appreciated. My nervousness also affects the dynamic with my manager, as my reticence and insecurity prevent me from setting clear communication or expectations. At the same time, I feel that I do not receive the support from my colleagues in this situation that I would like.

Part 2: TO-BE Situation

External Conditions and Resources

In the situation I desire, I would like to continue working as an IT specialist in a motivating environment where I can fully utilize my abilities. I imagine being able to clearly demonstrate both my professional competence and my commitment in my work environment and receiving the necessary recognition for it. I wish for a leader who provides guidance in key situations without exerting pressure. At the same time, I want to be able to act independently of my manager's feedback, that is, to be less dependent on his affirmation. An ideal situation would be a more balanced relationship between what I achieve and the recognition I receive.

Psychological Processes

My goal is to remain calm and confident in key situations, even if I am unsure whether I have met all of my manager's requirements perfectly. Instead of being blocked by uncertainty, I want to learn to trust my own abilities and knowledge. I aim to fully utilize my intellectual resources even under pressure and to be less guided by nervousness and tension. In my ideal situation, I feel motivated and able to assess my work independently, without relying on external feedback.

Observable Behaviors

In the desired TO-BE situation, I present myself more calmly and confidently in key situations. My behavior is characterized by greater self-assurance and initiative, especially when I am faced with tasks where I am not sure if they meet expectations. I no longer compulsively seek affirmation, but instead proactively and independently approach my manager to discuss clear expectations and, if necessary, obtain feedback. My behavior is marked by more self-confidence and a more relaxed approach, which has a positive effect on my performance and well-being.

Actual Consequences

Through these behavioral changes, I hope to achieve an improvement in my emotional stability and job satisfaction. I imagine that this will enable me to handle my tasks with more composure and efficiency, which not only increases my performance but also positively influences my relationship with my manager. Overall, I want to experience a work environment in which I am able to realize my potential to the fullest despite high demands, without constantly relying on external recognition.

This report summarizes the information available so far and forms the basis for a further detailed analysis of your problem and goal description.

User

Thank you very much for your explanations. They have spontaneously triggered the following in me:

[I now recognize the connections in my situation more clearly. That does me good and gives me hope. However, I see some details somewhat differently.]

I am adopting your "structured report of the current and target situation" with the following modifications:

[Part 1: Current Situation

External conditions and resources]

I have been working as an IT specialist in a team with ten colleagues for three years. I generally enjoy my work and have a good relationship with my team. A month ago, our team got a new manager who exerts a lot of pressure through his leadership style. He takes good performance for granted and gives little to no recognition, even for positive results. Although I continue to carry out my tasks carefully and with commitment,

I feel that my efforts are not appreciated. What is particularly stressful is that I become uncertain in certain situations when I am not sure whether my work meets my manager's expectations.
Psychological processes
My main problem arises in key situations when I am working on complex tasks and am not sure if I have done everything correctly. In these moments, I feel very nervous and tense. Although I do my work to the best of my ability, the uncertainty about the expected results puts me under enormous pressure. In these key situations, I experience a kind of "key effect": my tension prevents me from fully utilizing my intellectual abilities, which further intensifies my frustration and uncertainty. The fear of negative feedback from my manager makes me even more tense and often leads to me being unable to express myself well and sometimes coming across as abrupt and dismissive.
Observable behaviors
When I am in one of these key situations, I am very tense and make mistakes more frequently. In addition, I am less able to attune to other people. My behavior is strongly influenced by the uncertainty as to whether my work meets expectations. This uncertainty is reflected in my less confident demeanor and my inner stress, which is also visible externally. Sometimes I withdraw or reject others abruptly when I feel I am not getting clear guidance. In conversations with my manager, I seek affirmation, which rarely comes.
Factual consequences
The effects of my behavior are twofold: On the one hand, I feel increasingly insecure, frustrated, and isolated, which impacts my performance and motivation. Although I continue to do good work, my ability to realize my full potential is limited in key situations. This leads to additional stress, as I live with the feeling that I am not sufficiently appreciated. My nervousness also affects the dynamic with my manager, as my reticence and uncertainty prevent me from setting clear communication or expectations. At the same time, I feel that I do not receive the support from my colleagues in this situation that I would wish for.

***

Part 2: Target Situation
External conditions and resources
In the situation I desire, I would like to continue working as an IT specialist in a motivating environment where I can fully utilize my skills. I imagine that I can clearly demonstrate both my professional competence and my commitment in my professional environment and receive the necessary recognition for it. I wish for a leader who provides guidance in key situations without exerting pressure. At the same time, I want to be able to act independently of my manager's feedback, that is, to be less dependent on his affirmation. An ideal situation would be a more balanced relationship between what I achieve and the recognition I receive.
Psychological processes
My goal is to remain calm and confident in key situations, even if I am unsure whether I have perfectly met all my manager's requirements. Instead of being blocked by uncertainty, I want to learn to trust my own abilities and knowledge. I aim to fully utilize my intellectual resources even under pressure and to be less guided by nervousness

and tension. In my ideal situation, I feel motivated and able to assess my work independently, without relying on external feedback.
Observable behaviors
In the desired target situation, I present myself more composed and confident in key situations. My behavior is characterized by greater self-assurance and initiative, especially when I am faced with tasks where I am not sure if they meet expectations. I no longer compulsively seek affirmation, but instead approach my manager actively and independently to discuss clear expectations and, if necessary, to obtain feedback. My behavior is marked by greater self-confidence and a more relaxed approach, which has a positive effect on my performance and well-being.
Factual consequences
Through these behavioral changes, I hope for an improvement in my emotional stability and job satisfaction. I imagine that this will enable me to handle my tasks with more composure and efficiency, which not only increases my performance but also positively influences my relationship with my manager. Overall, I want to experience a work environment in which, despite high demands, I am able to realize my full potential without constantly relying on external recognition.]

- Task 3: In-depth exploration of the "key effect" using immersive image work

User

I have chosen a suitable image for my "key effect," which I describe as follows:
[I chose the image because it aptly describes the mood I have been experiencing more and more frequently lately. In the image, I see a person who is not clearly recognizable in the fog. When I immerse myself in the image, I feel the deep sense of disorientation and despondency of this person. My gaze is especially drawn to the indistinct face of this person, and I hear within myself the words: "It just can't be like this!"]
First, tell me how the description of this image relates to the description of my "key effect," and second, make a suggestion for a correspondingly more precise description of my "key effect."

AI

Relationship between the image and the "key affect"

The image of a person in the fog symbolizes a strong sense of disorientation and emotional insecurity. This description closely matches the feelings you experience in your key situations. The fog represents ambiguity and a lack of direction, similar to the uncertainty you feel when you are unsure whether your performance meets your manager's expectations. The blurred face illustrates the difficulty of seeing yourself clearly, indicating that in these moments you are unable to recognize your strengths and abilities. This inner insecurity, which is intensified in the image by the words "It can't be like this!", reflects your emotional response in key situations. You feel trapped in a state of ambiguity, which impairs your intellectual abilities and leads to additional tension.

Refined description of the "key affect"

The "key affect" describes the state in which your emotional tension and insecurity in key situations become so strong that your intellectual abilities are blocked. This mainly occurs when you are confronted with complex tasks and are unsure whether your work meets expectations. Your insecurity leads to nervousness, which in turn limits your ability to perform at your best. In these moments, you feel disoriented and may react abruptly or withdraw, which makes communication with your manager more difficult and further increases your stress. This creates a vicious cycle in which your insecurity and fear of negative feedback further undermine your performance and self-confidence.

User

Thank you for your explanations. They have spontaneously triggered the following in me:
[I am surprised and deeply moved by the possible interconnections you have made me aware of.]
I am adopting your refined description of the "key affect" with the following modifications:
[The "key affect" describes the state in which my emotional tension and insecurity in key situations become so strong that my intellectual and social abilities are blocked. This mainly occurs when I am confronted with complex tasks and am unsure whether my work meets my manager's expectations. This creates a vicious cycle in which my insecurity and fear of negative feedback further undermine my performance, my communication skills, and above all, my self-confidence.]

- Task 4: In-depth exploration of the coaching goal using immersive image work

User

I have also selected a suitable image for my coaching goal, which I describe as follows:
[I chose the image because it stands for openness, vastness, and optimism. In the image, I see a sea with a rising sun and a few delicate clouds. When I immerse myself experientially in the image, I feel the fresh sea air. My gaze is mainly drawn to the vastness of the sea ahead of me, and I hear the words within me: "Look at all that lies ahead of you!"]
First, tell me how the description of this image relates to the description of my coaching goal, and second, suggest a correspondingly refined description of my coaching goal.

AI

Relationship between the image and your coaching goal

The image of a vast sea with a rising sun symbolizes optimism, openness, and the possibility of discovering new paths. The sea stands for the infinite possibilities and the vastness of life, while the rising sun represents the beginning of a new day, that is, an opportunity for a fresh start. In relation to your coaching goal, the image reflects the desire to look beyond your current insecurity and to utilize the internal and external resources available to you. The fresh sea air symbolizes clarity and new energy that will accompany you on your path to greater self-confidence, performance, and communication skills. The image reinforces the focus on an open and future-oriented attitude, enabling you to let go of insecurities and face challenges with courage.

Refined description of your coaching goal

My coaching goal is to remain calm and self-assured in key situations and to purposefully overcome my insecurities. I want to learn to fully utilize my intellectual and social abilities even under pressure and to be less dependent on my manager's feedback. My goal is to trust in my own competencies, communicate clearly, and actively seek feedback in order to assess my performance independently and confidently. In doing so, I aim to strengthen my performance and self-confidence so that I can act not only professionally but also communicatively with confidence in complex tasks. Ultimately, I want to experience a work environment in which I can realize my potential without internal blockages and with an open, optimistic attitude.

- Task 5: Reconstruction of the "vicious cycle" using systemic constellation work

User

I conducted an in-depth interview with my coach based on the Inner Team model. The aim of the interview is to clarify, with regard to the "key situation," which of my personality parts support my coaching goal and which cause the "key affect" that hinders or prevents the pursuit and achievement of this goal.

[Speaker 1: Hello, Work Pride, what do you think of the team leader's goal to develop more self-confidence? Speaker 2: I think it's great. It's about time, too. With our qualifications and the quality of our work, we should be making a much bigger impact. Speaker 1: And you, Self-Criticism, what do you think? Speaker 2: I think it's totally problematic. I always say: Pride comes before a fall. We should really keep a low profile. What Work Pride always wants is far too risky in my opinion.]

Assume that the tensions between these two personality parts, as clearly shown in the transcribed in-depth interview, illuminate the core area of the present coaching issue. Therefore, use the "vicious cycle" text module to reconstruct the problem-stabilizing "vicious cycle" of the present coaching issue. In doing so, refer both to the transcribed interview and to all individual details of the present coaching issue.

AI

The problem-stabilizing "vicious cycle" of your coaching issue can be well reconstructed using the model of the Inner Team and the dynamics between the personality parts that become visible in your in-depth interview. The focus here is particularly on the conflict between **pride in your work** and **self-criticism,** which act as opposing poles and play a central role in your "key situation".

1. **Vicious cycle of the coaching issue**
   The conflict between pride in your work and self-criticism creates an inner tension that triggers the "key effect" and impairs your ability to act confidently and assuredly in key situations.
   - **Pride in your work** supports your coaching goal. It wants you to present yourself confidently and acknowledge your achievements, because your work is of high quality. This part demands that you become more self-assured and draw more attention to yourself. It stands for pride in your achievements and the desire to show them externally. However, this pride is blocked by **self-criticism.**
   - **Self-criticism,** on the other hand, reacts to the desire for pride in your work with caution and skepticism. It warns against becoming too self-confident, out of fear that this could lead to mistakes. The belief "pride comes before a fall" dominates this part. This part ensures that you hold back, doubt yourself, and question your abilities in order to avoid disappointment or setbacks.

These opposing impulses form the core of the **vicious cycle:**
- In a **key situation** where you are unsure whether your performance meets expectations, your self-confidence is undermined by your inner self-criticism. This uncertainty leads to emotional tension, which negativcly affects your intellectual and social abilities.
- Self-criticism perceives the uncertainty and amplifies it by fueling your fear of negative feedback. This causes you to focus more on possible criticism and less on your actual competencies and achievements.
- Avoiding self-confidence out of fear of mistakes not only blocks your coaching goal, but also reduces your ability to communicate clearly and confidently. This further increases the uncertainty, and the "key effect" occurs: your intellectual and social abilities are blocked in this situation.

2. **How the vicious cycle is stabilized**
   - **Selective perception:** Self-criticism filters your perception of your achievements selectively and focuses on possible weaknesses or risks. This selective perception increases uncertainty and reduces your ability to recognize successes or progress.
   - **Reinforcement through behavior:** As a result, you hesitate to act confidently or to highlight your achievements. This hesitation confirms the inner self-criticism that restraint is the safer path, which in turn frustrates pride in your work and further increases your uncertainty.
   - **Consequences in the social environment:** This dynamic impairs your communication with your manager, as you do not actively seek feedback or set clear expectations. This uncertainty in communication leads to a lack of recognition, which further increases your uncertainty and keeps the vicious cycle going.

The **vicious cycle** is thus stabilized by the mutual reinforcement of uncertainty and self-criticism, which undermines your self-efficacy and communication skills in key situations.

User

Thank you very much for your explanations. They have spontaneously triggered the following in me:
[A truly impressive analysis. I am beginning to understand my issue and myself better and better. I have no further questions – and I accept your analysis without modifications.]

- Assignment 6: Reconstruction of the central balancing problems

User

Please analyze, using the text module "balancing problems" as well as the other uploaded text modules, which balancing problems are at the core of my coaching issue.

AI

At the center of your coaching issue are various balancing problems that intensify your "key effect" and stabilize the vicious cycle. Using the text module "balancing problems", the following central conflicts can be identified:

1. **Security vs. Risk-taking**

In key situations, a dominant need for security becomes apparent. You hesitate to take bold steps and prefer to stay in familiar territory to avoid mistakes and negative feedback. This striving for security inhibits your ability to confidently take on new challenges.

2. **Process orientation vs. Results orientation**

You tend to get lost in processes instead of focusing on clear results. This leads you to engage intensively with the details of a task without making success measurable. This lack of results orientation increases your uncertainty in key situations.

3. **Need for recognition vs. Egocentrism**

Your need for recognition conflicts with the fear of standing out too much or being perceived as arrogant. This inner tension between the desire to show your achievements and the fear of rejection blocks your self-efficacy.

4. **Rationality vs. Intuition**

You rely heavily on rational decisions and neglect your intuitive judgment. In key situations, this leads you to postpone decisions for too long or to be guided by uncertainties instead of trusting your gut feeling.

5. **Self-exploitation vs. Self-preservation**

There is a tendency toward self-exploitation, where you try to meet your high expectations while simultaneously protecting yourself from overload. This tension leads you to overexert yourself while at the same time trying to conserve your resources.

Conclusion:

The dominant balancing problems concern your ability to take risks, focus clearly on results, and find a healthy approach to recognition and self-criticism. These unbalanced forces intensify the "key effect" and prevent you from fully realizing your potential.

User

Thank you very much for your explanations. They have spontaneously triggered the following in me, and I am adopting your analysis with the following modifications:

[Very stimulating analysis. I find some of the terms in the headings not entirely appropriate. This applies especially to the words "egocentrism" and "protective attitude." However, the descriptions underneath fit very well.]

Inspired by your analysis, I see that the following balancing issues underlie my problem:

[Most important balancing issue: striving for recognition vs. egocentrism

My need for recognition conflicts with the fear of standing out too much or being perceived as arrogant. This inner tension between the desire to demonstrate your performance and the fear of rejection blocks your self-efficacy.

Second most important balancing issue: self-exploitation vs. protective attitude

There is a tendency toward self-exploitation as I try to meet my high expectations without simultaneously protecting myself from overload. This tension leads me to overexert myself and not pay enough attention to conserving my resources.

Third most important balancing issue: security vs. risk-taking

In key situations, a dominant need for security becomes apparent. I hesitate to take bold steps and prefer to stay in familiar territory to avoid mistakes and negative feedback. This desire for security inhibits my ability to confidently take on new challenges.]

Task 7: Identification of the most important complementary forces

User

Using the text module "complementary forces," tell me which complementary forces I should strengthen in order to better balance these balancing issues.

AI

To address your balancing issues, you can strengthen certain **complementary forces** that will help you find a better equilibrium. Based on the balancing issues you have identified, these are the relevant complementary forces:

1. **Striving for recognition vs. egocentrism**
   - **Complementary force: Strengthening self-recognition.** You should use your own perception and evaluation as a reference point for your self-management. This means becoming emotionally more independent from the recognition of others and developing a socially balanced self-recognition.
2. **Self-exploitation vs. protective attitude**
   - **Complementary force: Conserving your own resources.** Make sure to protect your material, psychological, and physical resources more carefully in order

to avoid self-exploitation. This means developing a mindful optimization of your resource usage.

3. **Security vs. risk-taking**
   - **Complementary force: Courage to face challenges.** To balance the desire for security, you should gradually develop risk-tested courage by approaching challenging tasks more boldly. This will enable you to explore risks in a controlled manner and expand your scope for action.

By strengthening these complementary forces, you will create a better balance between the internal conflicts that make up your coaching issue.

User

Thank you very much for your explanations. They have spontaneously triggered the following in me:
[You are absolutely right. But the thing about self-recognition really doesn't sit well with me. Somehow I don't want to admit it, even though I know it's true.]

8

- Task 8: Development of a success imagination

User

Describe as precisely as possible in one—and really only one—sentence the "mental gold nugget activity" that will enable me to practically achieve the targeted strengthening of certain complementary forces.
Describe the consequences of this positive change in a personal experiential narrative written in the first person. I want to use this as a success imagination from now on.
In this success imagination, describe everything in a very differentiated, vivid, and personal way, so that it can be imagined as concretely as in a film—everything that happens externally and everything that happens intrapsychically within me. The experiential narrative starts with the "key situation," which has not changed. So, base the description on the "key situation" that I shared with you at the beginning of this chat. In the description of the success imagination, also refer to the two images I chose for my current and desired situation.
In this sense, create two clearly different experiential descriptions.

AI

Mental Gold Nugget Activity:
In key situations, I consciously focus on my own abilities, take a deep breath, acknowledge uncertainty as a temporary feeling, and make a courageous decision to actively tackle the task without fear of making mistakes.

First Experience Narrative (Success Imagination 1):

I am sitting at my desk, working with concentration on a complex task. Although I am unsure whether everything is correct, I take a moment, close my eyes, and picture the image of a person in the fog—a symbol of my uncertainty. But instead of letting this image paralyze me, I take a deep breath and visualize the fog lifting. I feel the freshness of the sea air on my face and see the vast ocean before me, with the rising sun on the horizon. The words "Look at all that lies ahead of you!" echo in my mind, and I feel a new sense of clarity. My nervousness transforms into calm determination as I continue working on the task. When my manager comes by, I remain composed. I meet them with an upright posture, actively ask for feedback, and take it as an opportunity for improvement, without letting their words intimidate me. I feel that I can trust my own abilities, and my thoughts focus on the positive opportunities ahead. I notice that I do not need recognition to know my worth—I know that I am competent. In this moment, my inner calm is tangible, and the emerging clarity gives me the confidence to master the task with poise.

Second Experience Narrative (Success Imagination 2):

The key situation begins as always: I am working on a difficult task and am not sure whether it meets my manager's expectations. My stomach tightens, and I feel the fog of uncertainty thickening in my mind. But instead of losing control, I recall the image of the rising sun over the sea. I visualize the image in my mind's eye, hear the wind, feel the salty air on my skin, and let the sense of vastness flow into me. "Look at all that lies ahead of you," I say to myself internally. The fog begins to clear, and my thoughts become more focused. Instead of concentrating on possible mistakes, I think about the many opportunities ahead. The uncertainty remains, but it no longer controls me. When my manager appears and asks about progress, I stay calm. I explain my thoughts without fear of having done something wrong. I feel empowered because I know I am doing my job well—even without constant external validation. Internally, I feel the tension subside, and a pleasant warmth spreads within me as I continue to work, focused and full of confidence that I will accomplish the task.

User

I am adopting your suggestions for the Gold Nugget Activity with the following modifications:

[In key situations, I consciously focus on my own abilities, take a deep breath, greet uncertainty kindly when it appears, and assign it a place that is a little further away from me. This way, I feel free and secure, able to decide courageously which tasks I will tackle next, actively and with optimism.] In the coming days, I want to try to carry out problem-solving actions that will help me achieve my coaching goal as quickly and sustainably as possible. The focus of these problem-solving actions must be the recently identified mental "Gold Nugget Activity." Therefore, I am instructing you to offer me three—but really only three and no more—meaningful problem-solving actions in this sense. They must be as concrete as possible and closely aligned with the information provided about my current coaching issue.

- Task 9: Identification of the next goal-oriented activities

AI

Here are three concrete problem-solving actions to help you apply your mental "Gold Nugget Activity" in key situations and move closer to your coaching goal:

1. **Conscious Preparation for Key Situations through Visualization**
   Before each complex task or important meeting, take five minutes to sit quietly, breathe deeply, and imagine the image of the vast sea with the rising sun. Visualize yourself remaining calm in the situation, welcoming uncertainty, and consciously assigning it a place "further away" before you courageously decide what to do next.
2. **Actively Seeking Feedback without Emotional Attachment**
   In a key situation, deliberately approach your manager to obtain constructive feedback on your work. Enter the conversation with the mindset that the feedback will help you develop further, without it affecting your self-worth. Consciously observe how you kindly set aside uncertainties in order to make confident decisions.
3. **Daily Reflection on the Implementation of the Gold Nugget Activity**
   At the end of each workday, take 10 minutes to reflect on the key situations of the day. Write down when and how you applied your mental Gold Nugget Activity—when you succeeded in welcoming uncertainty and consciously setting it aside—and note the positive effects you experienced.

8

User

Based on your suggestions, I am planning the following problem-solving activities for the next few days:
[Daily reflection on the implementation of the Gold Nugget Activity
At the end of each workday, I will take 10 minutes to reflect on the key situations of the day. I will write down when and how I applied my mental Gold Nugget Activity—that is, when I succeeded in welcoming uncertainties and consciously setting them aside—and I will note the positive effects I have observed.] Please save this without any comment. I will get back to you in the next few days and let you know how well the implementation went.

AI

Understood. I have saved your planned problem-solving activity without comment. I look forward to hearing from you about how the implementation went.

- Task 10: Implementation Support

User

In implementing my planned problem-solving activities, I had the following success experience:
[With a few exceptions, the evening documentation of the experiences I had that day with my Gold Nugget Activity went well. Although it was sometimes a bit painful to see again that carrying out the Gold Nugget Activities was often difficult for me and did not work out properly, the documentation itself went well and helped me make good progress.]

In implementing my planned problem-solving activities, I had the following failure experience:
[On two evenings, I thought about documenting but did not do it because I felt so ashamed. On those two days, I fell back into my old pattern and fully experienced the old stress and all the uncertainty again. That was not pleasant.]
Tell me what I can learn from the perspective of the "mental Gold Nugget Activity" of my success imagination and—where applicable—from my previous successes, so that I can be more successful in similar situations in the future. Please also use the text modules "Success Factors" and "Complementary Forces."

AI

Learning from Success Imagination and Previous Successes:

1. **Welcoming Uncertainty with the Gold Piece Activity**

An important lesson from your previous implementation is that it can sometimes be challenging to consistently apply the Gold Piece Activity, especially when uncertainty is high. One way to improve this is to **see uncertainty not as an obstacle, but as a companion**—something you consciously acknowledge, but keep at a friendly distance. This is a **complementary force** to the excessive focus on external feedback and the need for validation (recognition-seeking). It helps to strengthen your ability for **self-regulation** by using your own perception as the starting point for decisions.

2. **Steps Toward Self-Care and Realistic Expectations**

Self-exploitation in the form of high expectations of yourself can also be an obstacle. Here, it is crucial to find a balance between high performance standards and conserving your own resources. This means **being kinder to yourself and accepting small setbacks as learning opportunities.** The complementary force you can strengthen here is **mindful self-care,** where you use your resources responsibly and consciously incorporate moments of rest.

3. **Courage for Small Risks and Learning Tasks**

Your experience of failure shows that the need for security often prevails and makes bold decisions more difficult. To be more successful, you can start to take **small, controlled risks.** In key situations, this means deliberately embracing uncertainty and making decisions even if they are not completely risk-free. This complementary force strengthens the **courage to face challenges,** where uncertainty is seen not as a threat, but as an opportunity for growth.

Through these strategies, you can amplify the positive effects of your previous successes and continue to develop greater self-confidence and more assured actions.

User

Thank you very much for your explanations. I fully agree with your recommendations without any modifications:
Please save this without any comment. I will get back to you in the next few days and let you know how things have progressed.

References

Geißler H (2024) KI-Coaching. Die neue Generation der Coaching-Medien. Trainingaktuell Mai 2024, S 11–14, Bonn: ManagerSeminare

Helwig P (1967) Charakterologie. Herder, Freiburg im Breisgau

Schulz von Thun F (1989) Miteinander reden – 2 – Stile, Werte und Persönlichkeitsentwicklung. rororo, Reinbek bei Hamburg

Terblanche N (2024) Artificial Intelligence (AI) coaching: redefining people development and organizational performance. J Appl Behav Sci:1–8. ▸ https://doi.org/10.1177/00218863241283919

A Look into the Future

Contents

H. Geissler, *AI-Coaching*,
https://doi.org/10.1007/978-3-658-49178-9_9

No one can see into the future. However, it is possible to identify the most important current drivers of development and to reconstruct the logic of the present dynamics, assuming that these dynamics will also shape the future. (See also the future outlooks by Novic 2024, p. 350 ff.; Terblanche 2024, p. 107 f.; Rutschmann 2024, p. 366).

If we look at the current present in this sense, it becomes clear that the strongest driver of development is that traditional coaching—not only face-to-face coaching, but also online coaching—is increasingly coming under pressure to be displaced by AI, both through coaching AI agents and through non-coaching-specific chatbots such as ChatGPT, which are used as advisors.

There is much to suggest that this trend will continue and even intensify significantly. It is to be expected that the *user-friendliness* (usability) of these chatbots or AI agents will improve, especially through the expansion of oral communication capabilities, and that corresponding applications will therefore become constant companions, i.e., buddies, for many people in a wide variety of personal and professional situations.

This improvement in user-friendliness will go hand in hand with an improvement in *learning capability.* If a user tells an AI agent in detail every day what they experience, what moves them, and perhaps also what troubles them, and then gives the AI agent differentiated feedback, sharing how they perceive and implement its assessments and suggestions, this will generate chats that provide the AI agent with extremely rich material to tailor itself precisely to the characteristics and perspectives of the coachees.

It is to be expected—or feared—that this development will be driven by *economic interests* in such a way that there will be free or extremely low-priced offerings where users pay with their data and must therefore expect that this data will be used or misused for certain marketing purposes. On the other hand, there will also be higher-priced offerings characterized by high content quality, as the applications have differentiated access to domain-specific knowledge. For example, one might think of AI coaching for learning difficulties, job interviews, onboarding for a new position, dealing with difficult colleagues and supervisors, managing relationships with life partners, parenting, aging, and much more.

These *dyadic coaching* offerings can easily be upgraded by providing different models, including the option of additional support from a human coach if needed.

To optimize this interface also in terms of cost, it makes sense for coachees to allow their AI apps to communicate with the corresponding AI apps of their coaches. In this way, coaches can be very well informed about their coachees even before the first coaching session, thereby optimizing the cost-benefit ratio of these coaching engagements.

This development will also influence the *training* and *supervision* of coaches. It is to be expected that the capabilities of AI will be used in coach training for practicing conversation management skills and hypothesis formation based on diagnostics, and that coaches—just like the majority of people—will have an AI app as a personal companion, i.e., as a business buddy or as a supervisor for their professional concerns.

Of course, this does not preclude coaches from also working with human supervisors. However, even in this collaboration, corresponding AI apps will play an important role.

References

Novic H (2024) Rocky AI. In: Passmore J, Diller SJ, Isaacson S, Brantl M (Hrsg) The Digital and AI Coaches' handbook. Routledge, London/New York, S 349–352

Rutschmann R (2024) evoach. In: Passmore J, Diller SJ, Isaacson S, Brantl M (Hrsg) The Digital and AI Coaches' handbook. Routledge, London/New York, S 365–366

Terblanche N (2024) Artificial intelligence coaching chatbots. In: Passmore J, Diller SJ, Isaacson S, Brantl M (Hrsg) The Digital and AI Coaches' handbook. Routledge, London/New York, S 101–109

GPSR Compliance
The European Union's (EU) General Product Safety Regulation (GPSR) is a set of rules that requires consumer products to be safe and our obligations to ensure this.

If you have any concerns about our products, you can contact us on

ProductSafety@springernature.com

In case Publisher is established outside the EU, the EU authorized representative is:

Springer Nature Customer Service Center GmbH
Europaplatz 3
69115 Heidelberg, Germany

www.ingramcontent.com/pod-product-compliance
Lightning Source LLC
Chambersburg PA
CBHW070405041125
34948CB00019B/345
* 9 7 8 3 6 5 8 4 9 1 7 7 2 *